The All Color
Busy Cook's Book

The All Color
Busy Cook's Book

edited by
Margaret Empson

octopus

Contents

Notes

All recipes serve 4 people unless otherwise stated.

Standard spoon measurements are used in all recipes.
1 tablespoon = one 15ml spoon
1 teaspoon = one 5ml spoon
All spoon measures are level.

Fresh herbs are used unless otherwise stated. If unobtainable substitute a bouquet garni of the equivalent dried herbs, or use dried herbs instead but halve the quantities stated.

Plain (all-purpose) flour should be used unless otherwise stated.

Ovens should be preheated to the specified temperature.

Only one column of measures should be followed; the columns are not interchangeable.

First published 1979
by Octopus Books Limited
59 Grosvenor Street, London W1

© 1979 Octopus Books Limited
ISBN 0 7064 1065 3

Produced by Mandarin Publishers Limited
22a Westlands Road,
Quarry Bay, Hong Kong

Printed in Hong Kong

Introduction

Eating fresh home-cooked food is a pleasure but finding the time to prepare it may seem impossible, especially to the professional woman and the working mother With simple planning and carefully chosen dishes, even the most hectic lifestyle can cope with these difficulties.

All the recipes in this book – whether for the family or for entertaining – have been carefully selected for the busy woman. Each chapter contains a variety of favourite and new dishes which are easy to prepare – even within the busiest schedule. Although preparation and cooking can be done in advance, this is little help if you are always short of time. With this in mind the chosen recipes are all simple and quick to prepare. Shopping too, can be time-consuming, but you will find the necessary ingredients are readily available and can either be bought during the weekly 'shop' and stored until required, or fetched on the way home from work.

Planning your meals may seem dull but it only takes a little extra effort and is well worthwhile. The prepared cook generally enjoys cooking and does not find it a chore. Planning can mean batch baking – cooking several dishes at once in the oven – which saves fuel, as well as time. Dishes should be covered tightly after cooking and stored in the refrigerator until required.

Make full use of your refrigerator. Prepare green vegetables at the weekend: wash and drain thoroughly, then without crushing, store in sealed polythene bags or in roomy plastic boxes. Pop salad items in the salad drawer and they will keep well for several days. Store root vegetables in a cool airy place, where they will keep for at least a week.

Meat should be cooked soon after buying, especially minced (ground) meat. Whole pieces of lamb and beef can be stored uncooked in the refrigerator for 1 or 2 days: remove the shop wrappings, place the meat on a plate and cover completely with fresh plastic cling film. Cook fresh poultry as soon as possible;

frozen poultry must be thawed completely before cooking. All fresh fish should be cooked very soon after purchasing.

A home freezer can save time, especially if you plan carefully. When making a casserole or pie, prepare enough for two or three meals. Freeze the ones you are not using immediately and reheat as required. Although most frozen dishes can be reheated from solid, it's a good idea to transfer them to the refrigerator the night before you intend to serve them, or allow to thaw at room temperature so they will take less time to reheat – saving time and fuel. Recipes which are especially suitable for the freezer have instructions for freezing and thawing. Something to remember – if you intend to make the most of your freezer – don't freeze prepared dishes for too long as it is an expensive use of space.

There are other, less expensive, gadgets to assist you. Crockpots, or slow-cookers make superbly tender casseroles, tasty soups and other dishes too. They can be switched on before leaving for work and you return to a ready-cooked meal. Pressure cookers cut down on cooking time which can be very useful, especially for making stocks and steamed puddings. A hand-held mixer beats cake mixtures and egg whites quickly, but you probably won't rummage in a cupboard for one, so keep it readily accessible on a working surface. An electric blender or liquidizer is another useful labour-saving device for making puréed soups, pâtés or breadcrumbs, if kept handy. It's useful, too, for making salad dressing, dips and baby foods. When buying a blender, choose one with a generous capacity, otherwise you will waste time processing ingredients in small quantities.

The essential item for quick food preparation is a really sharp knife that's the right size for the task. Money spent on a small selection of really good quality knives is a better investment than a whole kitchen full of gadgetry!

Stock your storecupboard with useful items which will stretch a meal, such as pasta and rice, canned tomatoes and fish, stock (bouillon) cubes, dried fruits, whole nuts and unsweetened canned fruits – especially cherries, pineapple and apricots.

For flavour and cheapness, the best buys are always the vegetables and fruits which are in season. Out of season items may be available, but they're expensive. Very fresh vegetables need very little cooking and should be served immediately, lightly seasoned and tossed in a little butter. These are the best accompaniments to meat or fish and can be prepared in a flash. Potatoes take a little longer to cook but don't ignore the many and varied ways this versatile vegetable can be served: boiled, mashed, creamed, jacket-baked, roasted, sautéed, deep-fried, or turned into potato cakes or croquettes.

With fruits, too, enjoy them in season. You can afford to be generous with the quantities and you will enjoy those with a short season most! We're lucky to have fine imported citrus fruits and although they're available all the year round make the most of them during the winter months when soft fruit is unobtainable. Serve plain or transform them into Oranges in Caramel, Grapefruit Medley or Lemon Soufflé.

A troublefree dessert is a selection of fresh firm fruits served with cheese, or soft fruits with thin cream. Another easy dessert is poached fruits. Pears, apples, apricots, rhubarb, gooseberries and blackcurrants may all be poached, and served with thin cream or egg custard, they make a delicious conclusion to a meal. However, most of us like to prepare something a little special for a dinner party dessert and you will find recipes in this book which can be prepared in advance.

When entertaining it is advisable to prepare at least two of the courses ahead of time, such as the main course and the dessert, then assemble the starter just before the guests arrive. This order is essential if the starter is a salad. Once your guests arrive you will want to be with them. The hostess who chooses a simple meal, which can almost take care of itself, will enjoy her role and the evening to the full — especially when she is complimented on her cooking.

Compliments are not what you expect from the family, but clean plates will please you! Children may not like fussy food, but present them with a chicken casserole garnished with triangles of toast and they will love it. Individual pies are always more special than one big one, too. Perhaps you shouldn't encourage yourself or your family to eat snacks but homemade biscuits and cakes are irresistible and full of wholesome ingredients.

You'll enjoy cooking the dishes in this book because they permit you to be creative without taking up too much of your precious time.

Snacks and suppers

The working wife has neither time nor energy to prepare elaborate supper dishes or snacks so all recipes in this chapter have been carefully selected to keep both preparation and cooking time to a minimum. The ingredients are readily obtainable and can be purchased either during the weekly 'shop' or on the way home. Some of the recipes, even though they are quick to make, can be prepared in advance and stored in the refrigerator until required. Don't be surprised at the inclusion of savoury soufflés – although they have the reputation for being difficult to make – they can be prepared quickly especially if you have a hand mixer.

Crispy fried vegetables with garlic mayonnaise

METRIC/IMPERIAL
500 g/1 lb vegetables
oil for deep frying
Batter:
2 eggs, separated
300 ml/½ pint beer
25 g/1 oz butter, melted
175 g/6 oz flour
salt and pepper
½ teaspoon dried thyme
Mayonnaise:
150 ml/¼ pint mayonnaise
2 tablespoons fresh double cream
2 garlic cloves, crushed
1 teaspoon chopped fresh marjoram or
    parsley
AMERICAN
1 lb vegetables
oil for deep frying
Batter:
2 eggs, separated
1¼ cups beer
2 tablespoons butter, melted
1½ cups flour
salt and pepper
½ teaspoon dried thyme
Mayonnaise:
⅔ cup mayonnaise
2 tablespoons heavy cream
2 garlic cloves, minced
1 teaspoon chopped fresh marjoram or
    parsley

Use a variety of vegetables for this dish. Choose aubergines (eggplant), celeriac, cauliflower florets, Jerusalem artichokes, celery, fennel, parsnip, etc, cut into suitable sized pieces and steamed or boiled until half cooked before finishing; or mushrooms, sliced courgettes (zucchini), spring onion (scallion) bulbs, etc, can be fried from raw.

Make the batter: Mix the egg yolks and beer together. Stir in the butter and beat in the flour until the mixture is smooth. Whisk the egg whites until stiff and fold carefully into the batter with the salt, pepper and thyme.

For the mayonnaise, mix all the ingredients together adding salt and pepper to taste. Spoon into a serving dish.

Heat the oil to 180–190°C/350–375°F, dip each piece of vegetable into the batter, making sure it is covered completely and fry until golden brown and crisp. Drain on kitchen paper and keep warm in the oven.

Serve the vegetables with the mayonnaise, together with a selection of cold meats and salad, if liked.

Potted mushrooms

METRIC/IMPERIAL
75 g/3 oz butter
500 g/1 lb mushrooms, chopped
½ teaspoon dried basil
salt and pepper
AMERICAN
⅓ cup butter
1 lb mushrooms, chopped
½ teaspoon dried basil
salt and pepper

Melt 25 g/1 oz/2 tablespoons of the butter in a saucepan, add the mushrooms, basil and seasoning to taste. Cover the pan and cook very slowly for 10 minutes. Using a slotted spoon lift out the mushrooms and chop them very finely. Reduce the liquid in the pan until 2 tablespoons remain. Mix this with the mushrooms and check the seasoning. Press the mushroom mixture into 4 individual dishes and level the surface. Leave until cold.

Melt the remaining butter, skim the froth from the surface and pour into the dishes to cover the mushrooms. Leave until set. Serve as a starter with hot toast or crusty bread.

Prepare ahead. Cover the dishes with plastic wrap and chill in the refrigerator until 15 minutes before required.

Crispy fried vegetables with garlic mayonnaise; Potted mushrooms

Individual spinach soufflés

METRIC/IMPERIAL
15 g/½ oz butter
15 g/½ oz flour
100 g/4 oz chopped or puréed spinach
3 tablespoons fresh single cream
salt and pepper
¼ teaspoon grated nutmeg
50 g/2 oz Cheddar or Parmesan cheese, grated
2 eggs, separated

AMERICAN
1 tablespoon butter
2 tablespoons flour
½ cup chopped or puréed spinach
3 tablespoons light cream
salt and pepper
¼ teaspoon grated nutmeg
½ cup grated Cheddar or Parmesan cheese
2 eggs, separated

Melt the butter in a large saucepan, stir in the flour and cook for 1 minute. Add the spinach and stir in the cream and seasoning to taste. Bring the mixture to the boil and simmer gently for 1 minute. The mixture should be thick. Remove the pan from the heat and stir in the nutmeg, cheese and egg yolks, one at a time.

Beat the egg whites until stiff and fold carefully into the spinach mixture with a metal spoon. Spoon the mixture into 4 greased individual dishes and bake in a moderately hot oven, 200°C/400°F, Gas Mark 6 for 15 to 20 minutes or until firm on top and golden brown. Serve immediately.

Corn chowder: Individual spinach soufflés

Corn chowder

METRIC/IMPERIAL
50 g/2 oz bacon, chopped
1 small onion, chopped
3 medium potatoes, diced
300 ml/½ pint hot water
salt and pepper
500 g/1 lb sweetcorn
15 g/½ oz cornflour
900 ml/1½ pints milk
¼ teaspoon ground allspice or grated
    nutmeg
AMERICAN
¼ cup chopped bacon
1 small onion, chopped
3 medium potatoes, diced
1¼ cups hot water
salt and pepper
3 cups corn kernels
2 tablespoons cornstarch
3¾ cups milk
¼ teaspoon ground allspice or grated
    nutmeg

Cook the bacon in a saucepan over low heat until the fat runs. Add the onion and cook for 5 minutes or until soft. Add the potatoes, water and seasoning, cover and cook for 15 minutes or until the potatoes are almost cooked. Add the sweetcorn (kernels) and cook for a further 5 minutes.

Mix the cornflour (cornstarch) to a smooth paste with a little of the milk and add to the potato mixture. Add the remaining milk and the allspice or nutmeg and, stirring constantly, bring the mixture to the boil. Cook for 3 minutes, pour into warmed individual bowls and serve immediately.

Prepare ahead. Complete the cooking, cool, pour into a container and chill in the refrigerator. Reheat slowly and serve very hot.

Courgette (zucchini) and cheese bake

METRIC/IMPERIAL
50 g/2 oz butter
700 g/1½ lb courgettes, thickly sliced
1 teaspoon dried basil
1 teaspoon lemon juice
salt and pepper
100 g/4 oz spring onions, sliced
175 g/6 oz Mozzarella or other soft
    cheese, thinly sliced
50 g/2 oz dried breadcrumbs
AMERICAN
¼ cup butter
1½ lb zucchini, thickly sliced
1 teaspoon dried basil
1 teaspoon lemon juice
salt and pepper
¼ lb scallions, sliced
6 oz Mozzarella or other soft cheese,
    thinly sliced
½ cup dried breadcrumbs

Melt half the butter in a large saucepan, add the courgettes (zucchini) and cook for 10 minutes, stirring occasionally, until just tender. Remove the pan from the heat and add the basil, lemon juice, salt and pepper to taste and the spring onions (scallions). Mix well.

Butter a shallow ovenproof dish. Put in half the courgettes (zucchini) mixture, cover with half the cheese and repeat layers. Melt the remaining butter and fry the breadcrumbs until golden brown. Spread on top of the cheese and bake in a moderate oven, 180°C/350°F, Gas Mark 4 for 20 minutes or until the cheese has melted and the top is deep golden brown. Serve very hot with grilled (broiled) tomatoes.

Freeze. Wrap, seal, label and freeze. Thaw in a moderate oven, 180°C/350°F, Gas Mark 4 for 40 minutes or until heated through and crisp.

Leek pie

METRIC/IMPERIAL
275 g/10 oz plain flour
½ teaspoon salt
65 g/2½ oz butter
65 g/2½ oz shortening
about 2 tablespoons water
Filling:
350 g/12 oz leeks, cut into 2.5 cm/
    1 inch lengths
50 g/2 oz butter
2 egg yolks
2 tablespoons fresh double cream
4 slices bacon, grilled and crumbled
salt and pepper
AMERICAN
2½ cups flour
½ teaspoon salt
⅓ cup butter
⅓ cup shortening
about 2 tablespoons water
Filling:
¾ lb leeks, cut into 1 inch lengths
¼ cup butter
2 egg yolks
2 tablespoons heavy cream
salt and pepper
4 bacon slices, broiled and crumbled

Sift the flour and salt into a large bowl. Rub in the butter and shortening and mix to a firm dough with the water. Line a 20 cm/8 inch flan tin (pan) with two-thirds of the pastry.

Put the leeks and butter in a saucepan with 1 tablespoon water, cover and cook gently for 7 minutes or until the leeks begin to soften. Beat the egg yolks into the cream and stir into the leeks. Season to taste and cool slightly.

Pour the leek mixture into the pastry case, sprinkle over the bacon, and cover with the remaining pastry. Dampen the edges of the pastry with a little water and press together to seal. Make three small cuts in the centre of the pastry.

Bake the pie in a moderately hot oven, 200°C/400°F, Gas Mark 6 for 25 to 35 minutes or until the pastry is crisp and golden brown. Serve immediately as a light main dish.

Freeze. Do not cook; wrap, seal, label and freeze. Thaw in a very hot oven, 230°C/450°F, Gas Mark 8 for 30 minutes, then reduce to moderate, 180°C/350°F, Gas Mark 4 and bake for a further 30 minutes or until hot and lightly browned.

Beans and eggs au gratin

METRIC/IMPERIAL
500 g/1 lb shelled broad beans
3 hard-boiled eggs, sliced
40 g/1½ oz butter
40 g/1½ oz flour
450 ml/¾ pint milk
salt and pepper
pinch of cayenne pepper
Topping:
15 g/½ oz butter
25 g/1 oz fresh white breadcrumbs
50 g/2 oz Cheddar cheese, grated
AMERICAN
1 lb shelled lima beans
3 hard-cooked eggs, sliced
3 tablespoons butter
⅓ cup flour
2 cups milk
salt and pepper
pinch of cayenne pepper
Topping:
1 tablespoon butter
½ cup fresh white breadcrumbs
½ cup grated Cheddar cheese

Cook the beans in boiling salted water until just tender. Drain. Place a layer of beans in an ovenproof dish, scatter over half the egg slices, repeat layers and finish with a layer of beans.

Melt the butter in a saucepan, stir in the flour and cook for 1 minute. Gradually add the milk, stirring constantly, until the sauce is smooth. Add salt and pepper to taste and the cayenne pepper and bring the sauce to the boil, stirring. Cook for 2 minutes and pour over the beans.

Melt the butter and stir in the breadcrumbs. Sprinkle over the sauce and top with the grated cheese. Bake in a hot oven, 220°C/425°F, Gas Mark 7 for 15 minutes or until the topping is golden brown and the sauce bubbling.

Serve immediately as a light supper dish.

Note. If you wish to make the dish more substantial, add a can of drained tuna to the sauce.

Pipérade

METRIC/IMPERIAL
50 g/2 oz butter
1 tablespoon oil
1 medium onion, sliced
1 medium red or green pepper, seeded, cored and sliced
2 garlic cloves, crushed
3 large tomatoes, peeled, seeded and chopped
salt and pepper
4 eggs
2 tablespoons fresh single cream
Garnish:
bread triangles, toasted
1 garlic clove, crushed
about 25 g/1 oz butter
AMERICAN
¼ cup butter
1 tablespoon oil
1 medium onion, sliced
1 medium red or green pepper, seeded, cored and sliced
2 garlic cloves, minced
3 large tomatoes, peeled, seeded and chopped
salt and pepper
4 eggs
2 tablespoons light cream
Garnish:
bread triangles, toasted
1 garlic clove, minced
about 2 tablespoons butter

Melt the butter with the oil in a large saucepan. Add the onion and cook for 5 minutes or until soft. Add the peppers, garlic and tomatoes, season to taste, and simmer for 15 to 20 minutes or until the mixture is fairly thick.

Beat the eggs, cream and seasoning together and cook in a small saucepan until lightly scrambled.

Transfer the vegetable mixture to a heated serving dish. Pile the scrambled egg mixture into the centre. Mix together the garlic and butter and spread over the toast. Serve immediately as an unusual first course or as a light supper dish.

Note. If preferred, allow the dish to cool completely and serve cold, replacing the toast with French bread.

Pipérade: Beans and eggs au gratin

Spring onion (scallion) rarebits

METRIC/IMPERIAL
25 g/1 oz butter
225 g/8 oz Cheddar cheese, grated
few drops Tabasco sauce
salt and pepper
4 tablespoons brown ale
6 spring onions, chopped
freshly toasted bread
AMERICAN
2 tablespoons butter
2 cups grated Cheddar cheese
few drops Tabasco sauce
salt and pepper
4 tablespoons beer
6 scallions, chopped
freshly toasted bread

Melt the butter in a saucepan, stir in the cheese, Tabasco, salt and pepper to taste, beer and spring onions (scallions) and heat until smooth and creamy, stirring constantly. Do not allow the mixture to boil.

Spread the mixture on the toast and place under a hot grill (broiler) until golden and bubbling.

Serve immediately as a warming supper dish followed by fresh fruit.

Mushroom risotto

METRIC/IMPERIAL
1 medium onion, sliced
75 g/3 oz butter
4 slices bacon, rind removed and chopped
225 g/8 oz brown rice
750 ml/1¼ pints chicken stock
225 g/8 oz mushrooms, sliced
2 tablespoons chopped fresh parsley
½ teaspoon dried marjoram
salt and pepper
50 g/2 oz Parmesan cheese, grated
AMERICAN
1 medium onion, sliced
⅓ cup butter
4 bacon slices, rind removed and chopped
1¼ cups brown rice
3 cups chicken stock
2 cups sliced mushrooms
2 tablespoons chopped fresh parsley
½ teaspoon dried marjoram
salt and pepper
½ cup grated Parmesan cheese

Fry the onion in 50 g/2 oz/¼ cup of the butter until golden brown, add the bacon and rice and cook for 5 minutes, stirring. Pour in about a quarter of the stock, add the mushrooms, parsley and marjoram and cook until the liquid has been absorbed. Gradually add the remaining stock and simmer until the rice is just soft, about 25 to 30 minutes, and the liquid absorbed. Season the mixture well and stir in half the Parmesan cheese and the remaining butter.

Transfer the mixture to a warm serving dish and sprinkle with the remaining cheese. Serve immediately as a satisfying supper dish.

Potato and cheese casserole

METRIC/IMPERIAL
1 kg/2 lb potatoes, very thinly sliced
500 g/1 lb onions, thinly sliced
225 g/8 oz Cheddar cheese, thinly sliced
25 g/1 oz butter, cut into small pieces
½ teaspoon dried marjoram
salt and pepper
300 ml/½ pint milk
AMERICAN
2 lb potatoes, very thinly sliced
1 lb onions, thinly sliced
½ lb Cheddar cheese, thinly sliced
2 tablespoons butter, cut into small pieces
½ teaspoon dried marjoram
salt and pepper
1¼ cups milk

Place the potato slices in a large bowl of cold water and leave for 15 minutes. Drain thoroughly and dry roughly with absorbent kitchen paper.

Butter a shallow ovenproof dish and cover the base with a layer of potato slices. Cover with a layer of onion, then with a layer of cheese. Dot with a little butter, sprinkle with a little marjoram and season. Repeat these layers until all the ingredients are used up finishing with a layer of potatoes.

Heat the milk in a saucepan and bring to the boil. Pour the milk over the potatoes. Bake in a moderately hot oven, 190°C/375°F, Gas Mark 5 for 40 minutes or until the potatoes are tender when pierced with a skewer. Serve hot with a mixed salad or a green vegetable.
Freeze. Wrap, seal, label and freeze. Thaw in hot oven, 220°C/425°F, Gas Mark 7 for 20 minutes, then reduce to moderately hot, 190°C/375°F, Gas Mark 5 and cook for a further 40 minutes until heated through.

Chicory (endive) au gratin

METRIC/IMPERIAL
6–8 heads of chicory
6–8 slices smoked bacon, rinds removed,
    or 6–8 slices ham
25 g/1 oz butter
25 g/1 oz flour
300 ml/½ pint milk
100 g/4 oz Cheddar, Gruyère or
    Parmesan cheese, grated
1 teaspoon prepared French mustard
¼ teaspoon dried thyme
2 tablespoons fresh double cream
    (optional)
salt and pepper
AMERICAN
6–8 heads of endive
6–8 bacon slices, rinds removed, or 6–8
    slices ham
2 tablespoons butter
¼ cup flour
1¼ cups milk
1 cup grated Cheddar, Gruyère or
    Parmesan cheese
1 teaspoon prepared French mustard
¼ teaspoon dried thyme
2 tablespoons heavy cream (optional)
salt and pepper

Blanch the chicory (endive) in boiling
water for 10 minutes, drain and leave to
cool slightly. Wrap each head in a slice of
bacon or ham.

Butter a shallow ovenproof dish and
place the chicory (endive) over the base
of the dish, packing them closely
together.

Melt the butter in a saucepan, add the
flour and cook for 1 minute. Gradually
add the milk, stirring constantly, and
bring the sauce to the boil, still stirring.
Simmer for 1 minute. Add all but 2
tablespoons of the cheese, the mustard,
thyme, cream (if using) and salt and
pepper to taste. Pour the sauce over the
chicory (endive) and sprinkle over the
remaining cheese.

Bake in a moderately hot oven,
190°C/375°F, Gas Mark 5 for 20
minutes or until bubbling and golden
brown on top.

Freeze. Do not cook; wrap, seal, label and
freeze. Thaw in a hot oven, 220°C/
425°F, Gas Mark 7 for 20 minutes,
reduce to moderate, 180°C/350°F, Gas
Mark 4 and bake until heated through
and browned on top.

Ham soufflé; Chicory (endive) au gratin

Ham soufflé

METRIC/IMPERIAL
50 g/2 oz butter
1 small onion, finely chopped
40 g/1½ oz flour
150 ml/¼ pint fresh single cream
4 egg yolks
175 g/6 oz lean ham, chopped
salt and pepper
5 egg whites
AMERICAN
¼ cup butter
1 small onion, finely chopped
⅓ cup flour
⅔ cup light cream
4 egg yolks
¾ cup chopped lean cooked ham
salt and pepper
5 egg whites

Melt the butter in a large saucepan, add the onion and cook gently for 5 minutes or until soft but not browned. Stir in the flour and cook for 1 minute. Gradually stir in the cream. Bring the mixture slowly to the boil, stirring all the time. Remove the pan from the heat and stir the egg yolks quickly into the mixture. Stir in the ham and season to taste.

Beat the egg whites until stiff and fold carefully into the ham mixture. Butter a 1 litre/2 pint/5 cup soufflé dish and pour in the ham mixture. Bake in a moderately hot oven, 190°C/375°F, Gas Mark 5 for 30 to 40 minutes or until the soufflé has risen and formed a crust. The centre should still be creamy. Serve immediately as an impressive first course or as a light supper dish.

Spinach roll

METRIC/IMPERIAL
175 g/6 oz spinach, fresh or frozen
salt and pepper
175 g/6½ oz cheese, grated
4 eggs, separated
25 g/1 oz butter
50 g/2 oz button mushrooms, sliced
25 g/1 oz flour
300 ml/½ pint milk
AMERICAN
6 oz spinach, fresh or frozen
salt and pepper
1½ cups grated cheese
4 eggs, separated
2 tablespoons butter
½ cup sliced small mushrooms
¼ cup flour
1¼ cups milk

Spinach roll

Grease and line a 28 × 18 cm/11 × 7 inch Swiss (jelly) roll tin.

Cook the spinach in a little boiling water for 5 minutes or until tender. Drain thoroughly. Chop very finely or purée in an electric blender until smooth.

Mix together the spinach, salt and pepper to taste, 2 tablespoons of the cheese, and the egg yolks. Beat the egg whites until stiff and fold into the spinach mixture. Pour the mixture into the prepared tin and bake in a moderately hot oven, 190°C/375°F, Gas Mark 5 for 10 to 15 minutes or until springy when pressed with a fingertip.

Meanwhile, melt the butter, add the mushrooms and cook for 1 minute. Stir in the flour and cook for 1 minute. Gradually stir in the milk to make a smooth sauce. Bring to the boil, stirring, and cook for 2 minutes. Season to taste.

Turn out the spinach mixture onto a flat surface, spread with the sauce and roll up. Lift carefully onto a warmed serving dish and serve immediately with jacket potatoes.

Macaroni and cheese casserole

METRIC/IMPERIAL
50 g/2 oz butter or margarine
50 g/2 oz flour
¼ teaspoon dry mustard
600 ml/1 pint milk
175 g/6 oz well-flavoured Cheddar or
    other hard cheese, grated
salt and pepper
100 g/4 oz cut macaroni
25 g/1 oz dried breadcrumbs
15 g/½ oz butter, cut into small pieces to
    finish

AMERICAN
¼ cup butter or margarine
½ cup flour
¼ teaspoon dry mustard
2½ cups milk
1½ cups grated well-flavored Cheddar or
    other hard cheese
salt and pepper
1 cup elbow macaroni
¼ cup dried breadcrumbs
1 tablespoon butter, cut into small pieces
    to finish

Melt the butter or margarine in a sauce-pan, add the flour and mustard and cook for 1 minute. Add the milk gradually, stirring well after each addition, until the sauce is smooth and bring to the boil, stirring. Remove the pan from the heat and add all but 2 tablespoons of the cheese. Season to taste and keep warm.

Cook the macaroni according to package directions in plenty of boiling salted water until just tender, about 10 minutes. Drain, rinse in cold water and drain again. Butter an ovenproof dish, put in a layer of macaroni, pour over a thick layer of sauce, repeat layers. Mix together the remaining cheese and the breadcrumbs and sprinkle over the sauce. Dot the butter over the top and bake in a moderately hot oven, 190°C/375°F, Gas Mark 5 for 20 minutes or until bubbling and golden brown.

Serve immediately with beans and carrots.

Pizza

METRIC/IMPERIAL
225 g/8 oz plain flour
2½ teaspoons baking powder
½ teaspoon salt
40 g/1½ oz butter or margarine
150 ml/¼ pint milk
500 g/1 lb tomatoes, thinly sliced
1 × 50 g/1¾ oz can anchovy fillets,
    drained
½ teaspoon dried basil
75 g/3 oz Mozzarella, or other soft
    cheese, thinly sliced
pepper
25 g/1 oz black olives, halved and stoned
oil for sprinkling

Macaroni and cheese casserole; Pizza

AMERICAN
2 cups flour
2½ teaspoons baking powder
½ teaspoon salt
3 tablespoons butter or margarine
⅔ cup milk
1 lb tomatoes, thinly sliced
1 × 1¾ oz can flat anchovies, drained
½ teaspoon dried basil
3 oz Mozzarella, or other soft cheese,
    thinly sliced
pepper
⅓ cup ripe olives, halved and pitted
oil for sprinkling

Sift the flour, baking powder and salt into a bowl. Rub in the butter or margarine and stir in the milk to make a soft, but not sticky, dough. Divide the dough in half and press each into a 23 cm/9 inch circle on 1 or 2 baking sheets.

Cover the circles with the tomato slices. Make a lattice of anchovies on top and sprinkle with the basil. Arrange the cheese slices on top, sprinkle with pepper to taste and scatter over the olive halves. Sprinkle the topping with a little oil and bake in a hot oven, 220°C/425°F, Gas Mark 7 for 20 to 25 minutes or until the base is cooked and the topping is golden brown.

Cut the pizzas in halves or quarters and serve immediately.

Pissaladière

METRIC/IMPERIAL
4 tablespoons olive oil
700 g/1½ lb onions, chopped
1 sprig thyme
1 teaspoon dried mixed herbs
salt and pepper
2 garlic cloves, crushed
1 × 50 g/1¾ oz can anchovy fillets,
  drained
25 g/1 oz black olives, halved and stoned
Pastry:
225 g/8 oz flour
½ teaspoon salt
50 g/2 oz shortening, cut into small
  pieces
50 g/2 oz butter or margarine, cut into
  small pieces
about 2 tablespoons water
AMERICAN
4 tablespoons olive oil
1½ lb onions, chopped
1 sprig thyme
1 teaspoon dried mixed herbs
salt and pepper
2 garlic cloves, minced
1 × 1¾ oz can flat anchovies, drained
⅓ cup ripe olives, halved and pitted
Pastry:
2 cups flour
½ teaspoon salt
¼ cup shortening, cut into small pieces
¼ cup butter or margarine, cut into small
  pieces
about 2 tablespoons water

Heat 3 tablespoons of the oil in a large saucepan and cook the onions very gently for 10 minutes or until they are very soft and a rich golden colour. Stir in the herbs, seasoning and garlic and cook gently for a further 5 minutes.

Meanwhile, sift the flour and salt into a mixing bowl. Add the shortening and butter or margarine and rub in until the mixture resembles fine breadcrumbs. Add enough water to make a stiff dough. Roll out the dough and line a 20 cm/8 inch flan tin (pan). Trim the edges and bake 'blind' in a moderately hot oven, 200°C/400°F, Gas Mark 6 for 15 minutes or until cooked but not coloured. Transfer the pastry case to a baking sheet.

Transfer the onion mixture to the pastry case, make a lattice pattern on top with the anchovies and arrange the olives in the squares. Sprinkle over the remaining oil and bake in a moderately hot oven for 10 minutes or until really hot. Serve immediately.

Prepare ahead. Make and bake the pastry case, cool completely and wrap in aluminium foil until required. Cook the onion mixture, place in a suitable container, cover, cool and chill until required. Reheat in a moderately hot oven for 25 to 30 minutes or until very hot.

Pissaladière

Tuna and olive pie

METRIC/IMPERIAL
100 g/4 oz flour
½ teaspoon salt
50 g/2 oz shortening, cut into small
   pieces
about 1 tablespoon water
Filling:
25 g/1 oz butter
1 small onion, finely chopped
1 × 210 g/7½ oz can tuna fish, flaked
50 g/2 oz cheese, grated
2 tomatoes, peeled and chopped
few drops Tabasco sauce
10 stuffed olives, sliced
pepper
½ teaspoon dried mixed herbs
AMERICAN
1 cup flour
½ teaspoon salt
¼ cup shortening, cut into small pieces
about 1 tablespoon water
Filling:
2 tablespoons butter
1 small onion, finely chopped
1 × 7½ oz can tuna fish, flaked
½ cup grated cheese
2 tomatoes, peeled and chopped
few drops Tabasco sauce
10 pimiento stuffed olives, sliced
pepper
½ teaspoon dried mixed herbs

Sift the flour and salt into a mixing bowl,
add the shortening and rub in until the
mixture resembles fine breadcrumbs.
Add enough water to make a stiff dough.
Knead lightly and chill while making the
filling.

Melt the butter in a saucepan, add the
onion and cook for 5 minutes or until soft
but not browned. Remove the pan from
the heat and stir in the tuna, cheese,
tomatoes, Tabasco, olives, salt and pepper to taste and herbs. Cool slightly and
place in an 18 cm/7 inch flan tin (pan).
Roll out the pastry to a circle slightly
larger than the tin (pan), cover the filling
and trim the edges. Use the trimmings to
decorate the pie.

Bake in a moderately hot oven,
200°C/400°F, Gas Mark 6 for 25 minutes or until the pastry is golden brown.
Serve the pie hot with broad (lima) beans
or courgettes (zucchini), and tomatoes.
Freeze. Do not cook; wrap, seal, label
and freeze. Thaw in a hot oven,
220°C/425°F, Gas Mark 7 for 25
minutes, reduce to moderately hot,
190°C/375°F, Gas Mark 5 for a further
40 minutes or until heated through,
golden brown and crisp.

Onion and cheese bake

METRIC/IMPERIAL
12 slices bread
50 g/2 oz butter, softened
2 tablespoons oil
3 medium onions, sliced
500 g/1 lb tomatoes, peeled and sliced
225 g/8 oz Gruyère cheese, grated
½ teaspoon dried marjoram
few drops Worcestershire sauce
3 eggs, beaten
600 ml/1 pint milk
salt and pepper
225 g/8 oz bacon slices, rinds removed
AMERICAN
12 slices bread
¼ cup butter, softened
2 tablespoons oil
3 medium onions, sliced
1 lb tomatoes, peeled and sliced
2 cups grated Gruyère cheese
½ teaspoon dried marjoram
few drops Worcestershire sauce
3 eggs, beaten
2½ cups milk
salt and pepper
½ lb bacon slices, rinds removed

Spread one side of the bread with the butter and line the base of a 1 litre/ 2 pint/5 cup ovenproof dish with a few slices.

Heat the oil in a frying pan (skillet) and fry the onion until golden brown. Arrange a layer of onion on the bread and cover with a layer of tomatoes. Sprinkle with some of the cheese, marjoram and Worcestershire sauce. Continue making layers; finish with a layer of bread and scatter over any remaining cheese.

Beat the eggs and milk together, season to taste and pour into the dish. Bake in a moderate oven, 180°C/350°F, Gas Mark 4 for 45 minutes or until set and golden brown.

Cut the bacon slices in half crossways, stretch them and roll up. Fry or grill (broil) them until crisp.

Serve the bake with the bacon rolls as a hearty supper dish.

Prepare ahead. Assemble the layers, pour in the egg mixture, cover the dish and chill in the refrigerator until required. Bake in a moderate oven for 55 minutes or until set and golden and serve as above.

Tuna and olive pie

Haddock with fennel and celery sauce

Haddock with fennel and celery sauce

METRIC/IMPERIAL
1 kg/2 lb fresh or frozen haddock or other
  white fish
65 g/2½ oz butter
salt and pepper
3 celery stalks, chopped
1 fennel head, chopped
600 ml/1 pint milk
50 g/2 oz flour
½ teaspoon dry mustard
25 g/1 oz Parmesan cheese, grated
Garnish:
lemon wedges
celery leaves
AMERICAN
2 lb fresh or frozen haddock or other white
  fish
⅓ cup butter
salt and pepper
3 celery stalks, chopped
1 fennel head, chopped
2½ cups milk
½ cup flour
½ teaspoon dry mustard
¼ cup grated Parmesan cheese
Garnish:
lemon wedges
celery leaves

Place the fish in a greased ovenproof dish, dot with 15 g/½ oz/1 tablespoon of the butter and season with salt and pepper.

Cook the celery and fennel in a saucepan of boiling salted water and cook for 5 minutes or until just tender. Drain and spoon over the fish. Pour in the milk, cover and cook in a moderate oven, 180°C/350°F, Gas Mark 4 for 12 minutes or until the fish is almost cooked.

Drain the cooking liquid from the fish and reserve. Melt the remaining butter in a pan, stir in the flour and cook for 1 minute. Gradually add the cooking liquid, stirring constantly, and bring to the boil, still stirring. Stir in the mustard and half the cheese. Pour over the vegetables and fish and sprinkle with the remaining cheese. Return the dish to the oven and cook for 15 minutes or until bubbling and lightly browned.

Serve immediately, garnished with the lemon wedges and celery leaves.
Serves 4–6.

Herb flan

METRIC/IMPERIAL

225 g/8 oz flour
½ teaspoon salt
50 g/2 oz shortening, cut into small
    pieces
50 g/2 oz butter or margarine, cut into
    small pieces
about 2 tablespoons water
Filling:
25 g/1 oz butter
1 medium onion, chopped
25 g/1 oz flour
300 ml/½ pint milk
100 g/4 oz Cheddar cheese, grated
salt and pepper
1 teaspoon of each of the following:
    chopped fresh marjoram, fennel, savory,
    chives, basil and thyme
2 eggs, separated

AMERICAN

2 cups flour
½ teaspoon salt
¼ cup shortening, cut into small pieces
¼ cup butter or margarine, cut into small
    pieces
about 2 tablespoons water
Filling:
2 tablespoons butter
1 medium onion, chopped
¼ cup flour
1¼ cups milk
1 cup grated Cheddar cheese
salt and pepper
1 teaspoon of each of the following:
    chopped fresh marjoram, fennel, savory,
    chives, basil and thyme
2 eggs, separated

Sift the flour and salt into a mixing bowl. Add the shortening and butter or margarine and rub in until the mixture resembles fine breadcrumbs. Add enough water to make a stiff dough. Roll out the dough and line a 20 cm/8 inch flan tin (pan). Trim the edges and bake 'blind' in a moderately hot oven, 200°C/400°F, Gas Mark 6 for 15 minutes or until cooked but not coloured. Transfer the pastry case to a baking sheet.

Meanwhile, melt the butter in a saucepan, stir in the onion and cook for 5 minutes until soft but not brown. Stir in the flour, cook for 1 minute then add the milk, stirring constantly. Bring the mixture to the boil, still stirring, and cook for 2 minutes. Cool slightly and stir in the cheese, seasoning to taste, herbs and egg yolks, mix well. Beat the egg whites until stiff and fold carefully into the sauce.

Pour the mixture into the pastry case and cook in a moderately hot oven for 25 to 30 minutes or until set and golden brown. Serve hot or cold.

Asparagus Flan. Omit the herbs. Arrange 225 g/½ lb well-drained, canned asparagus in the pastry case before pouring in the egg mixture.

Mediterranean baked fish

METRIC/IMPERIAL

25 g/1 oz butter
2 tomatoes, peeled and sliced
1 small green pepper, seeded and sliced
100 g/4 oz button mushrooms, sliced
salt and pepper
4 red mullet or other small whole fish,
    cleaned and trimmed
4 tablespoons red wine or stock
1 tablespoon chopped fresh chives

AMERICAN

2 tablespoons butter
2 tomatoes, peeled and sliced
1 small green pepper, seeded and sliced
1 cup sliced small mushrooms
salt and pepper
4 red snapper or other small whole fish,
    cleaned and trimmed
4 tablespoons red wine or stock
1 tablespoon chopped fresh chives

Above: Herb flan

Right: Mediterranean baked fish

Using half the butter, grease an ovenproof dish. Add the tomatoes, pepper and mushrooms, in layers, sprinkling with salt and pepper to taste. Lay the fish on top and season lightly. Pour over the wine or stock and dot the fish with the remaining butter.

Cover the dish and bake in a moderate oven, 180°C/350°F, Gas Mark 4 for 30 to 40 minutes or until the fish is tender and flakes easily. Serve the fish hot, sprinkled with chives.

Macaroni fish pie

METRIC/IMPERIAL
500 g/1 lb haddock fillet
juice of ½ lemon
salt and pepper
25 g/1 oz butter
225 g/8 oz cut macaroni
25 g/1 oz Cheddar cheese, grated
Sauce:
25 g/1 oz butter
25 g/1 oz flour
300 ml/½ pint milk
few drops Worcestershire sauce
50 g/2 oz Cheddar cheese, grated
parsley sprig to garnish
AMERICAN
1 lb haddock fillet
juice of ½ lemon
salt and pepper
2 tablespoons butter
2 cups elbow macaroni
¼ cup grated Cheddar cheese
Sauce:
2 tablespoons butter
¼ cup flour
1¼ cups milk
few drops Worcestershire sauce
½ cup grated Cheddar cheese
parsley sprig to garnish

Place the fish in an ovenproof dish, pour over the lemon juice, season and dot with the butter. Cover the dish and cook in a moderate oven, 180°C/350°F, Gas Mark 4 for 10 to 15 minutes or until just cooked.

Meanwhile, cook the macaroni in boiling salted water for 10 to 12 minutes or until just tender. Drain thoroughly.

In a saucepan melt the butter, stir in the flour and cook for 1 minute. Gradually add the milk, stirring constantly, to make a smooth sauce. Add the Worcestershire sauce to taste and bring the mixture to the boil, stirring, Stir in the cheese.

Remove any skin or bones from the fish and flake roughly. Stir the fish and macaroni into the sauce. Pour the mixture into a warmed ovenproof dish, sprinkle over the remaining cheese and place under a hot grill (broiler) for 3 minutes or until the top is bubbling and golden.

Garnish with the parsley and serve immediately as a warming supper dish.

Macaroni fish pie

Bouillabaisse

METRIC/IMPERIAL
700 g/1½ lb assorted fish (cod, haddock,
  whiting, plaice, halibut, snapper, red or
  grey mullet)
2 tablespoons olive oil
1 medium onion, chopped
2 small leeks, sliced
1 garlic clove, crushed
1 × 397 g/14 oz can tomatoes
few sprigs parsley, thyme and marjoram,
  tied together
salt and pepper
125 ml/¼ pint fish stock or water
large pinch of saffron (optional)
175 g/6 oz shellfish (shrimps, prawns,
  mussels)
chopped fresh fennel

AMERICAN
1½ lb assorted fish (cod, haddock, whiting,
  flounder, halibut, snapper, red or grey
  mullet)
2 tablespoons olive oil
1 medium onion, chopped
2 small leeks, sliced
1 garlic clove, minced
1 × 14 oz can tomatoes
few sprigs parsley, thyme and marjoram,
  tied together
salt and pepper
⅔ cup fish stock or water
large pinch of saffron (optional)
1 cup shellfish (shrimp, mussels, clams)
chopped fresh fennel

Cut the fish into bite-sized pieces and put
in a large ovenproof dish.

Heat the oil in a saucepan, add the
onion, leeks and garlic and fry for 5
minutes or until soft. Add the tomatoes
and the juice and bring the mixture to
the boil. Add the herbs, salt and pepper to
taste and the stock or water and pour
onto the fish. Place the dish in a moderately hot oven, 190°C/375°F, Gas
Mark 5 and cook for 30 minutes or until
the fish is almost cooked. Stir in the
saffron (if using) and the shellfish and
cook for a further 15 minutes or until
very hot. Discard the bunch of herbs.

Serve the fish sprinkled with the fennel
and accompanied by French bread.

Serves 4–6.

Bouillabaisse

Stuffed cauliflower

METRIC/IMPERIAL
1 large cauliflower
Filling:
25 g/1 oz butter
1 medium onion, chopped
225 g/8 oz lean minced beef
225 g/8 oz tomatoes, peeled and chopped
2 tablespoons tomato purée
salt and pepper
$\frac{1}{2}$ teaspoon dried mixed herbs
$\frac{1}{2}$ teaspoon sugar
1 tablespoon chopped fresh basil (optional)
50 g/2 oz rice, boiled until just tender
Sauce:
450 ml/$\frac{3}{4}$ pint milk
50 g/2 oz button mushrooms, sliced
25 g/1 oz butter
25 g/1 oz flour
1 teaspoon French mustard
100 g/4 oz Cheddar cheese, grated
AMERICAN
1 large cauliflower
Filling:
2 tablespoons butter
1 medium onion, chopped
1 cup lean ground beef
1 cup peeled and chopped tomatoes
2 tablespoons tomato paste
salt and pepper
$\frac{1}{2}$ teaspoon mixed dried herbs
$\frac{1}{2}$ teaspoon sugar
1 tablespoon chopped fresh basil (optional)
$\frac{1}{4}$ cup rice, boiled until just tender
Sauce:
2 cups milk
$\frac{1}{2}$ cup sliced small mushrooms
2 tablespoons butter
$\frac{1}{4}$ cup flour
1 teaspoon French mustard
1 cup grated Cheddar cheese

Cook the cauliflower in boiling salted water until almost cooked, about 8 minutes.

Meanwhile, melt the butter and fry the onion and meat until lightly browned. Add the tomatoes, purée (paste), seasoning, herbs, sugar and basil (if using). Simmer for 10 minutes then stir in the rice.

Meanwhile, heat the milk and mushrooms together and simmer for 5 minutes. Melt the butter in a saucepan, stir in the flour and cook for 1 minute. Gradually stir in the milk and mushrooms to make a smooth sauce. Bring the mixture to the boil, stirring, and cook for

Stuffed cauliflower

2 minutes. Remove the pan from the heat and stir in half the cheese.

Put the whole cauliflower in an oven-proof dish and cut downwards, almost completely through the stem, so it falls into quarters. Put the meat filling into the cuts. Coat the meat and cauliflower with the sauce and sprinkle the remaining cheese over the top. Bake in a moderately hot oven, 200°C/400°F, Gas Mark 6 for 15 minutes or until golden brown. Serve immediately, accompanied by crusty wholemeal bread.

Note. If the cauliflower falls to pieces as you cut it, cut it into florets and lay them in the dish, cover with the meat mixture and pour the sauce over. Sprinkle with the cheese and bake in the same way.

Meatballs Napoli

METRIC/IMPERIAL
700 g/1½ lb lean minced beef
2 small onions, very finely chopped
1 garlic clove, crushed
4 tablespoons dried breadcrumbs
1 egg, beaten
1 teaspoon dried marjoram
1 teaspoon chopped fresh fennel
salt and pepper
4 tablespoons flour
⅛ teaspoon cayenne pepper
oil for frying
397 g/14 oz can tomatoes, puréed or sieved
150 ml/¼ pint chicken stock
1 tablespoon red wine vinegar
1 teaspoon sugar
2 tablespoons grated Parmesan cheese
AMERICAN
1½ lb lean ground beef
2 small onions, very finely chopped
1 garlic clove, minced
4 tablespoons dried breadcrumbs
1 egg, beaten
1 teaspoon dried marjoram
1 teaspoon chopped fresh fennel
salt and pepper
4 tablespoons flour
⅛ teaspoon cayenne pepper
oil for frying
14 oz can tomatoes, puréed or sieved
⅔ cup chicken stock
1 tablespoon red wine vinegar
1 teaspoon sugar
2 tablespoons grated Parmesan cheese

Mix the beef with half the onions, the garlic and the breadcrumbs and stir in the egg to bind. Add half the marjoram and fennel, salt and pepper to taste and stir well.

Shape the meat mixture into about 30 balls and roll in the flour seasoned with the cayenne pepper.

Heat 2 tablespoons of oil in a large saucepan and brown the meatballs, a few at a time, on all sides. Remove and drain as they brown. Add more oil to the pan if necessary.

Add the remaining onion to the pan and fry gently until golden. Add the tomatoes, chicken stock, vinegar and sugar and the remaining herbs. Season to taste. Bring the mixture to the boil, stirring constantly, then lower the heat and return the meatballs to the pan. Cover and simmer very gently for 40 minutes or until cooked.

Pour the mixture into a warmed serving dish and sprinkle over the Parmesan cheese. Serve with freshly cooked spaghetti or other pasta and extra Parmesan cheese.

Freeze. Don't add Parmesan, wrap, seal, label and freeze. Thaw in covered container in a moderately hot oven, 190°C/375°F, Gas Mark 5 for about 1 hour or until heated through. Serve as above.

Swedish beef patties

METRIC/IMPERIAL
700 g/1½ lb lean minced beef
1 small onion, finely chopped
1 tablespoon capers, drained and finely chopped
½ teaspoon dried dill
2 medium cooked beetroot, finely chopped
1 large potato, boiled, skinned and mashed with 1 tablespoon butter and 2 tablespoons fresh double cream
salt and pepper
1 egg, beaten
oil for frying
AMERICAN
1½ lb lean ground beef
1 small onion, finely chopped
1 tablespoon capers, drained and finely chopped
½ teaspoon dried dill
2 medium cooked beets, finely chopped
1 large potato, boiled, skinned and mashed with 1 tablespoon butter and 2 tablespoons heavy cream
salt and pepper
1 egg, beaten
oil for frying

Put the beef, onion, capers, dill, beetroot (beets) and potato in a large bowl and mix well together. Season to taste and bind the mixture with the egg. Dip your hands in water and shape the mixture into 4 flat patties.

Fry the patties for about 5 minutes on each side if you like them medium cooked, a little longer if you like them well cooked.

Serve the patties with jacket potatoes and salad, or in warmed rolls garnished with onion and tomato slices and your favourite sauces.

Mediterranean-style pork chops

METRIC/IMPERIAL
25 g/1 oz butter
1 tablespoon oil
4 lean pork chops, trimmed of fat
350 g/12 oz mushrooms, sliced
2 large green or red peppers, seeded, cored and sliced
350 g/12 oz tomatoes, peeled and sliced
1 teaspoon each chopped fresh marjoram, sage and thyme
1 teaspoon sugar
salt and pepper
300 ml/½ pint chicken stock or water
AMERICAN
2 tablespoons butter
1 tablespoon oil
4 pork loin chops, trimmed of fat
3 cups sliced mushrooms
2 large green or red peppers, seeded, cored and sliced
¾ lb tomatoes, peeled and sliced
1 teaspoon each chopped fresh marjoram, sage and thyme
1 teaspoon sugar
salt and pepper
1¼ cups chicken stock or water

Heat the butter and oil together in a large saucepan. Add the chops and brown quickly on each side. Remove. Fry the mushrooms, peppers and tomatoes until soft. Stir in the herbs, sugar, seasoning and stock or water. Cover and simmer for 5 minutes. Return the chops to the pan and simmer, uncovered, for 30 minutes or until the chops are cooked right through. The sauce should be thick, but if it gets too thick during cooking add a little water.

Transfer the chops to a warm serving dish and serve with the sauce, accompanied by boiled rice.

Note. Lamb chops (rib or loin) may be used instead; trim away fat and reduce cooking time to 20 minutes.

Roman liver

METRIC/IMPERIAL
500 g/1 lb lambs' liver, cut into thin slices
25 g/1 oz flour
salt and pepper
25 g/1 oz butter
1 tablespoon oil
1 medium onion, finely chopped
1 garlic clove, crushed
1 teaspoon Worcestershire sauce
1 teaspoon dried mixed herbs
1 × 397 g/14 oz can tomatoes
AMERICAN
1 lb lamb liver, cut into thin slices
¼ cup flour
salt and pepper
2 tablespoons butter
1 tablespoon oil
1 medium onion, finely chopped
1 garlic clove, minced
1 teaspoon Worcestershire sauce
1 teaspoon dried mixed herbs
1 × 14 oz can tomatoes

Coat the liver in the flour seasoned with salt and pepper. Melt the butter in a large saucepan and fry the liver gently for 3 minutes, turning once, or until just cooked but still pink in the centre. Set aside.

Heat the oil in a saucepan, add the onion and garlic and fry for 5 minutes or until the onion is soft. Stir in any remaining flour, the Worcestershire sauce, herbs and tomatoes with their juice, and bring to the boil. Half cover the pan and simmer for 10 minutes or until slightly reduced.

When the sauce has thickened, add the liver and any juices and simmer for 3 minutes or until just heated through. Don't cook the liver too long or else it will be hard.

Serve the liver very hot with pasta.

Kidney and mushroom casserole

METRIC/IMPERIAL
700 g/1½ lb lambs' or calves' kidneys, skin and cores removed
75 g/3 oz butter
1 tablespoon oil
500 g/1 lb button onions, blanched and peeled or medium onions, quartered
500 g/1 lb button mushrooms
4 tablespoons port or Madeira
150 ml/¼ pint soured cream
salt and pepper
1 tablespoon chopped fresh chives
AMERICAN
1½ lb lamb or veal kidneys, skin and cores removed
⅓ cup butter
1 tablespoon oil
1 lb baby white onions, blanched and peeled or medium onions, quartered
1 lb small mushrooms
4 tablespoons port or Madeira
⅔ cup sour cream
salt and pepper
1 tablespoon chopped fresh chives

Cut the kidneys into thick slices. Heat the butter and oil in a large saucepan, add the kidneys and cook gently until they have browned on all sides. Transfer to a plate. Add the onions to the pan and brown quickly. Transfer to the plate. Add the mushrooms to the pan and cook until starting to soften. Transfer to the plate.

Pour the port or Madeira into the pan, increase the heat and bubble for 1 minute. Return the kidney mixture to the pan, cover and simmer very gently for 15 minutes or until the kidneys are tender. Stir in the sour(ed) cream, season to taste and pour into a warmed serving dish. Sprinkle with the chives and serve with freshly boiled rice and a green bean salad.

Roman liver

Cheese and onion soufflé

METRIC/IMPERIAL
50 g/2 oz butter
100 g/4 oz onion, very finely chopped
150 ml/¼ pint fresh single cream
4 egg yolks
100 g/4 oz Cheddar cheese, grated
salt and pepper
5 egg whites
AMERICAN
¼ cup butter
1 cup very finely chopped onion
⅔ cup light cream
4 egg yolks
1 cup grated Cheddar cheese
salt and pepper
5 egg whites

Melt the butter in a large saucepan, add the onion and cook over very low heat for 10 minutes or until very soft but not brown. In a bowl, beat together the cream and egg yolks until well mixed. Stir in the onion mixture and the cheese. Add seasoning to taste. Beat the egg whites until stiff and fold very carefully into the cheese mixture. Spoon into a buttered 1 litre/2 pint/5 cup soufflé dish and bake in a moderately hot oven, 190°C/375°F, Gas Mark 5 for 30 to 35 minutes or until well risen and golden and crusty looking, though the centre should still be creamy in texture.

Serve immediately as a splendid savoury starter or as a light supper dish followed by a selection of salads.

Curried chicken salad

METRIC/IMPERIAL
350 g/12 oz cooked chicken, chopped
1 tablespoon mild curry powder
1 garlic clove, crushed
150 ml/¼ pint mayonnaise
150 ml/¼ pint soured cream
1 green pepper, seeded, cored and chopped
½ cucumber, halved, seeded and chopped
1 tablespoon tomato purée
100 g/4 oz button mushrooms, sliced
salt and pepper
4 tomatoes, sliced, to garnish
AMERICAN
1½ cups chopped cooked chicken
1 tablespoon mild curry powder
1 garlic clove, minced
⅔ cup mayonnaise
⅔ cup sour cream
1 green pepper, seeded, cored and chopped
½ cucumber, halved, seeded and chopped
1 tablespoon tomato paste
1 cup sliced small mushrooms
salt and pepper
4 tomatoes, sliced, to garnish

Put the chicken, curry powder, garlic, mayonnaise and sour(ed) cream in a bowl, mix well and allow to stand for 30 minutes. Stir in the pepper, cucumber, tomato purée (paste), mushrooms and seasoning to taste and mix well. Pile the mixture onto a chilled serving dish and surround with the tomato slices.

Serve as part of a cold buffet or as a light supper dish in the summer, or winter if preceded by hot soup.

Italian pasta salad

METRIC/IMPERIAL
175 g/6 oz pasta shells
225 g/8 oz bacon slices, rinds removed and chopped
175 g/6 oz continental smoked garlic sausage, cut into 1 cm/½ inch pieces
175 g/6 oz black or green grapes, halved and pips removed
1 small red pepper, seeded, cored and sliced
Dressing:
120 ml/4 fl oz unsweetened yogurt
120 ml/4 fl oz fresh double cream
1 tablespoon chopped fresh marjoram or mint
1 tablespoon lemon juice
salt and pepper
AMERICAN
1½ cups pasta shells
1 cup chopped bacon
6 oz continental smoked garlic sausage, cut into ½ inch pieces
1½ cups black or green grapes, halved and seeded
1 small red pepper, seeded, cored and sliced
Dressing:
½ cup unsweetened yogurt
½ cup heavy cream
1 tablespoon chopped fresh marjoram or mint
1 tablespoon lemon juice
salt and pepper

Cook the pasta in boiling salted water for 10 to 12 minutes or until just tender. Drain. Fry the bacon over low heat until the fat runs, increase the heat and fry until crisp. Drain on absorbent kitchen paper. Put the pasta, bacon, garlic sausage, grapes and pepper in a bowl and mix well.

Put the yogurt, cream, herb, lemon juice and salt and pepper to taste in a bowl and beat until thoroughly mixed. Pour over the pasta mixture and stir well. Pile into a serving dish.

Serve as a lunch or supper dish accompanied by a tomato and a green salad.

Cheese and onion soufflé

Main meals to cook ahead

Tasty, tender casseroles are the main-stay of this chapter but in every recipe the preparation time has been kept to a minimum and the ingredients are readily available. You will need plenty of storecupboard items – pasta, tomato purée (paste) and canned fish and vegetables – so keep a stock of these. None of the dishes are expensive because most of them are based on the cheaper cuts of meat and vegetables.

Casseroles are marvellous for busy people; the ingredients are quickly prepared and the dish can be forgotten for an hour or two while it's cooking. One or two freshly-cooked vegetables are the only accompaniments needed. If you haven't time to prepare potatoes for the meal, remember rice and pasta require no preparation, cook quickly and go with most dishes. Crusty fresh bread is another alternative – but if you are slimming you can forget about any of these accompaniments!

Although the dishes in this chapter are essentially practical, this shouldn't stop you serving them when entertaining. You can easily turn a main dish into something a little special by garnishing attractively and serving with a wider selection of vegetables and a glass of wine.

All of the dishes in this chapter can either be served immediately, or prepared in advance and reheated quickly. If you are not serving straight away, cool the dishes quickly, then store in the refrigerator. Reheat thoroughly before serving. One word of warning: casserole dishes cannot be hurried, so when planning your meal allow plenty of cooking time and use that time to do what you want to do.

Tuna loaf

METRIC/IMPERIAL
1 × 198 g/7 oz can tuna fish, drained and flaked
100 g/4 oz fresh white breadcrumbs
¼ teaspoon grated nutmeg
½ teaspoon chopped fresh fennel
salt and pepper
125 ml/¼ pint milk
1 egg, beaten
4 tomatoes, sliced
100 g/4 oz Cheddar cheese, grated

AMERICAN
1 × 7 oz can tuna fish, drained and flaked
2 cups fresh white breadcrumbs
¼ teaspoon grated nutmeg
½ teaspoon chopped fresh fennel
salt and pepper
⅔ cup milk
1 egg, beaten
4 tomatoes, sliced
1 cup grated Cheddar cheese

Mix together the fish, breadcrumbs, nutmeg, fennel, seasoning to taste, milk and egg and beat well. Place a layer of tomatoes in the base of a 500 g/1 lb loaf tin (pan), cover with half the cheese and half the fish mixture; make another layer of tomatoes and cheese and finish with the remaining fish mixture, smoothing the surface. Cover with aluminium foil and place in a baking tin half-filled with water.

Bake in a moderate oven, 160°C/325°F, Gas Mark 3 for 1 hour or until lightly set. Remove the tin (pan) from the water, release the loaf from the sides of the tin (pan) and turn out onto a warmed serving plate. Serve immediately with a leek and celery salad. If serving cold, leave the loaf to cool completely before turning out onto a chilled plate and serve with a green salad.
Prepare ahead. Leave to become completely cold, cover and chill in the refrigerator until required. Turn out and serve chilled.

Illustrated overleaf: Tuna loaf

Tuna loaf (page 31)

Vegetable lasagne

METRIC/IMPERIAL
4 tablespoons oil
500 g/1 lb onions, sliced
500 g/1 lb tomatoes, peeled and sliced
500 g/1 lb courgettes, sliced
2 garlic cloves, crushed
1 teaspoon dried marjoram
150 ml/¼ pint wine or stock
salt and pepper
8 sheets lasagne
50 g/2 oz butter
50 g/2 oz flour
600 ml/1 pint milk
1 teaspoon dry mustard
175 g/6 oz Cheddar cheese, grated

AMERICAN
4 tablespoons oil
1 lb onions, sliced
1 lb tomatoes, peeled and sliced
1 lb zucchini, sliced
2 garlic cloves, minced
1 teaspoon dried marjoram
⅔ cup wine or stock
salt and pepper
8 sheets lasagne
¼ cup butter
½ cup flour
2½ cups milk
1 teaspoon dry mustard
1½ cups grated Cheddar cheese

Heat 3 tablespoons of the oil in a large saucepan, add the onions and cook for 7 minutes or until soft and golden. Add the tomatoes and courgettes (zucchini) and cook, stirring, for a few minutes. Stir in the garlic, marjoram, wine or stock and salt and pepper to taste. Cover and simmer for 25 minutes or until the vegetables are very soft.

Meanwhile, cook the lasagne in boiling salted water with the remaining oil for 12 minutes or until just tender. Drain, keeping the sheets separate.

Melt the butter in a saucepan, stir in the flour and cook for 1 minute. Gradually stir in the milk to make a smooth sauce, bring to the boil, stirring constantly, and cook for 2 minutes. Stir in the mustard and two-thirds of the cheese.

Cover the base of an ovenproof dish with about one-third of the vegetable mixture, cover with a layer of lasagne, pour on some of the sauce, cover with lasagne, repeat the layers twice more but finish with a layer of sauce. Sprinkle over the remaining cheese and bake in a moderately hot oven, 190°C/375°F, Gas Mark 5 for 20 to 25 minutes or until bubbling and golden brown on top. Serve immediately.

Prepare ahead. Assemble the layers, sprinkle over the cheese and cool completely. Cover and chill in the refrigerator until required. Reheat in a moderately hot oven for 30 to 40 minutes or until bubbling and golden brown on top.

Smoked cod mousse

METRIC/IMPERIAL
225 g/8 oz smoked cod, cooked
15 g/½ oz powdered gelatine
150 ml/¼ pint chicken stock
2 tablespoons lemon juice
75 g/3 oz butter, melted
75 g/3 oz Edam or Gruyère cheese, cubed
salt and pepper
1 tablespoon chopped fresh chives
Garnish:
cucumber slices
lemon wedges
cress or lettuce

AMERICAN
½ lb smoked cod or other smoked white
  fish, cooked
2 packets gelatin
⅔ cup chicken stock
2 tablespoons lemon juice
⅓ cup melted butter
½ cup cubed Edam or Gruyère cheese
salt and pepper
1 tablespoon chopped fresh chives
Garnish:
cucumber slices
lemon wedges
cress or lettuce

Remove any bones and skin from the fish
and flake the flesh.

Sprinkle the gelatin(e) over the stock
and leave for 5 minutes. Place in a pan of
hot water and heat gently until the
gelatin(e) has dissolved. Place the fish,
gelatin(e) mixture, lemon juice, butter,
cheese and seasoning to taste in an
electric blender and blend until fairly
smooth. Taste and adjust seasoning, if
necessary. Stir in the chives and transfer
to a bowl or mould. Leave in a cool place
until set. Dip the bowl or mould in hot
water to loosen and turn out onto a
chilled serving plate. Garnish with the
cucumber slices, lemon and cress or
lettuce and serve with jacket potatoes
and salad.

Prepare ahead. Leave the mixture to set,
cover and chill until 15 minutes before
required. Turn out and garnish as above.

Smoked cod mousse

Stuffed aubergines (eggplant)

METRIC/IMPERIAL
2 large aubergines
salt
4 tablespoons oil
1 medium onion, finely chopped
4 tomatoes, peeled and chopped
1 garlic clove, crushed
½ teaspoon dried mixed herbs
pepper
150 ml/¼ pint stock
75 g/3 oz fresh white breadcrumbs
40 g/1½ oz Cheddar cheese, grated
15 g/½ oz butter
AMERICAN
2 large eggplant
salt
4 tablespoons oil
1 medium onion, finely chopped
4 tomatoes, peeled and chopped
1 garlic clove, minced
½ teaspoon dried mixed herbs
pepper
⅔ cup stock
1½ cups fresh white breadcrumbs
⅓ cup grated Cheddar cheese
1 tablespoon butter

Cut the aubergines (eggplant) in half and make shallow cuts on the cut surfaces. Sprinkle with salt and leave for about 20 minutes or until some of the juice comes out. Rinse the halves and pat dry with absorbent kitchen paper. Heat 3 tablespoons of the oil in a large pan and fry the aubergines (eggplant) until lightly brown on the cut sides. Remove the flesh leaving the skins intact. Chop the flesh. Fry the onion in the remaining oil until soft and mix with the aubergines (eggplant), tomatoes, garlic, herbs and salt and pepper to taste. Spoon into the aubergine (eggplant) skins. Place in an ovenproof dish and pour the stock around them.

Cook the aubergines (eggplant) in a moderate oven, 180°C/350°F, Gas Mark 4 for 30 to 40 minutes or until tender. Mix together the breadcrumbs and cheese and sprinkle over the aubergines (eggplant). Dot the top with butter and increase the temperature to moderately hot, 200°C/400°F, Gas Mark 6 and cook for a further 10 minutes or until the topping is crisp and golden. Alternatively, place the aubergines (eggplant) under a hot grill (broiler) until bubbling and golden brown. Serve hot as a starter or side dish with grilled (broiled) meat.

Prepare ahead. Cook until the aubergines (eggplant) are tender, cover, cool and chill in the refrigerator until required. Place the aubergines (eggplant) in a large saucepan, pour the cooking liquid around and bring to the boil. Cover tightly and simmer for 15 minutes or until hot. Place in a grill (broiler) pan, sprinkle over the breadcrumb and cheese mixture, dot with the butter and place under a hot grill (broiler) until bubbling and golden.

Stuffed aubergines (eggplant)

Vegetable cannelloni

METRIC/IMPERIAL
12 tubes cannelloni
500 g/1 lb tomatoes, peeled and chopped
100 g/4 oz Cheddar cheese, grated
100 g/4 oz fresh white breadcrumbs
1 tablespoon chopped fresh mixed herbs
salt and pepper
1 egg, beaten
15 g/½ oz butter
150 ml/¼ pint stock
AMERICAN
12 tubes cannelloni
1 lb tomatoes, peeled and chopped
1 cup grated Cheddar cheese
2 cups fresh white breadcrumbs
1 tablespoon chopped fresh mixed herbs
salt and pepper
1 egg, beaten
1 tablespoon butter
⅔ cup stock

Cook the cannelloni tubes in boiling salted water for 7 minutes or until almost tender. Drain well.

Mix together half the tomatoes, the cheese, breadcrumbs, herbs, salt and pepper to taste and the egg and beat well. Stuff the tubes with this mixture.

Grease an ovenproof dish with half the butter and lay the stuffed tubes in it. Scatter over the remaining tomatoes, season, and pour in the stock. Dot with the remaining butter and bake in a moderate oven, 180°C/350°F, Gas Mark 4 for 30 to 40 minutes or until the cannelloni and tomatoes are tender. Serve very hot accompanied by extra grated cheese and a green salad.
Prepare ahead. Cook the tubes, stuff and lay in the buttered dish. Add the remaining ingredients, cool, cover and chill in the refrigerator until required. Bake in a moderate oven for 40 to 50 minutes or until hot and bubbling.

Vegetable cannelloni

Dolmades

METRIC/IMPERIAL
4 tablespoons olive oil
1 medium onion, finely chopped
1 garlic clove, crushed
75 g/3 oz chicken livers
100 g/4 oz cooked rice
25 g/1 oz pine kernels
salt and pepper
36 canned vine leaves
about 300 ml/½ pint chicken stock
juice of 1 lemon to serve
AMERICAN
4 tablespoons olive oil
1 medium onion, finely chopped
1 garlic clove, minced
½ cup chicken livers
⅔ cup cooked rice
¼ cup pine kernels
salt and pepper
36 canned vine leaves
about 1¼ cups chicken stock
juice of 1 lemon to serve

Heat the oil in a saucepan and fry the onion and garlic for 5 minutes or until soft. Add the chicken livers and fry for 3 minutes, stirring, or until lightly browned on all sides. Remove the livers and chop finely. Place the rice in a bowl, stir in the livers, onion, garlic and pan juices, pine kernels and salt and pepper to taste until well mixed.

Lay the vine leaves on a board with the underside of the leaves uppermost. Put a teaspoonful of the rice mixture on each leaf and roll up, tucking the sides in as you do so to make a neat parcel. Place the leaves, close together so they don't unroll during cooking, in a casserole, making another layer or two if necessary.

Pour in enough stock to come half way up the sides of the casserole and just cover the leaves. Cover tightly and cook in a moderate oven, 180°C/350°F, Gas Mark 4 for 30 to 40 minutes or until very hot and cooked through.

Serve immediately, or allow to cool, and serve with the lemon juice.
Prepare ahead. Cover tightly and chill in the refrigerator until required. Serve immediately if serving cold or leave at room temperature for 30 minutes if you don't like dishes too chilled. Alternatively, reheat in a moderately hot oven, 190°C/375°F, Gas Mark 5 for 20 minutes or until heated through. Serve with the lemon juice.

Pork terrine

METRIC/IMPERIAL

1.25 kg/2½ lb belly pork, skinned, boned
and finely chopped
225 g/8 oz pig's liver, sliced
1 medium onion, very finely chopped
2 garlic cloves, crushed
1 tablespoon chopped fresh or 1 teaspoon
dried rosemary
1 egg
2 tablespoons brandy or dry sherry
salt and pepper
2 bay leaves to garnish

AMERICAN

2½ lb belly pork, finely chopped
½ lb pork liver, sliced
1 medium onion, very finely chopped
2 garlic cloves, minced
1 tablespoon chopped fresh or 1 teaspoon
dried rosemary
1 egg
2 tablespoons brandy or dry sherry
salt and pepper
2 bay leaves to garnish

Work the pork and liver together
through the fine blade of a mincer (grinder). Alternatively, purée the liver in an
electric blender and mix with the finely
chopped pork. Add the onion, garlic and
rosemary to the meat. Stir in the egg and
brandy or sherry and beat well to mix.
Season generously.

Spoon the mixture into a large terrine
or soufflé dish (1 litre/2 pint/5 cup) and
bake in a hot oven, 220°C/425°F, Gas
Mark 7 for 15 minutes. Reduce the heat
to moderately hot, 190°C/375°F, Gas
Mark 5 and bake for a further 1 to 1½
hours or until the meat has shrunk away
from the sides of the dish and the juices
run clear when the pâté is pierced with a
skewer.

Place a saucer or plate on the pâté and
weight it down. Leave in cool place until
cold. Remove the weights.

Garnish the pâté with the bay leaves
and serve with bread and salad as a main
dish.

Prepare ahead. Remove the weights,
garnish the pâté, cover the dish completely and chill in refrigerator until 30
minutes before required.

Freeze. After weighting and cooling,
wrap, seal, label and freeze. Thaw for 20
to 24 hours in the refrigerator or for 6 to
7 hours at room temperature.

Serves 6.

Dolmades

Illustrated overleaf: Country-style pâté

Country-style pâté

METRIC/IMPERIAL

25 g/1 oz butter
1 small onion, finely chopped
225 g/8 oz lambs' liver, cut into pieces
100 g/4 oz lean pork, cut into pieces
100 g/4 oz belly pork, sliced
1 garlic clove, crushed
½ teaspoon dried marjoram
salt and pepper
1 tablespoon dry sherry or brandy
100 g/4 oz lean streaky bacon

AMERICAN

2 tablespoons butter
1 small onion, finely chopped
½ lb lamb liver, cut into pieces
¼ lb lean boneless pork, cut into pieces
¼ lb unsalted fatty pork, sliced
1 garlic clove, minced
½ teaspoon dried marjoram
salt and pepper
1 tablespoon dry sherry or brandy
¼ lb bacon slices

Melt the butter in a frying pan (skillet)
and cook the onion and liver until the
liver is cooked but slightly pink in the
centre.

Place the liver on a board and chop
finely. Mince (grind) the pork, or chop it
finely in an electric blender, or chop it
finely with a sharp knife. Mix together
the onion, liver, pork, garlic, marjoram
and salt and pepper to taste. Add the
sherry or brandy and mix thoroughly.

Line a 500 g/1 lb loaf tin (pan) with
the bacon, fill with the pâté mixture and
cover with aluminium foil. Stand the tin
(pan) in a baking tin half-filled with hot
water and bake in a moderate oven,
180°C/350°F, Gas Mark 4 for 1¼ hours
or until the mixture is cooked through.

Allow the pâté to cool slightly in the
tin (pan), cover with fresh foil and
weight down until completely cold.

Turn out onto a serving plate and
serve cold, cut into slices with bread or
toast, and salad.

Prepare ahead. Turn out onto a clean
piece of aluminium foil, cover completely
and chill until 30 minutes before required. Serve as above.

Note. To cook in a slow cooker or crockpot, stand the tin (pan) in the pot with
enough hot water to come half way up
the sides of the tin (pan). Cook on low for
4–6 hours and leave to cool in the
container.

Freeze. Wrap, seal, label and freeze.
Thaw in the refrigerator for 24 hours or
at room temperature for 6 to 7 hours.

Stuffed Lambs' Hearts

METRIC/IMPERIAL
6 lambs' hearts
100 g/4 oz fresh white breadcrumbs
1 teaspoon each chopped fresh parsley,
    thyme and sage
1 egg
25 g/1 oz flour
salt and pepper
25 g/1 oz lard
1 medium onion, sliced
2 small carrots, sliced
2 stalks celery, sliced
300 ml/½ pint brown stock
1 tablespoon cornflour

AMERICAN
6 lambs' hearts
2 cups fresh white breadcrumbs
1 teaspoon each chopped fresh parsley,
    thyme and sage
1 egg
¼ cup flour
salt and pepper
2 tablespoons lard
1 medium onion, sliced
2 small carrots, sliced
2 stalks celery, sliced
1¼ cups brown stock
1 tablespoon cornstarch

Wash the hearts thoroughly. Trim away any fat, tubes or gristle and dry on absorbent kitchen paper.

Mix together the breadcrumbs and herbs and bind with the egg. Stuff the hearts with this mixture and sew up the opening. Roll the hearts in the flour seasoned with salt and pepper.

Melt the lard in a large saucepan and fry the hearts until lightly browned on all sides. Transfer to a casserole. Add the onion, carrots and celery to the fat and cook for 5 minutes or until the onion is soft. Add the stock and bring the mixture to the boil. Pour over the hearts, cover and bake in moderate oven, 160°C/325°F, Gas Mark 3 for 2 hours or until the hearts are tender. Transfer the hearts to a warmed serving dish, remove the string and keep warm.

Mix the cornflour (cornstarch) to a smooth paste with a little water. Pour the cooking liquid into a small pan, stir in the cornflour (cornstarch) mixture and bring to the boil, stirring; cook for 1 minute or until thick and clear. Pour the

*Stuffed lambs' hearts; Country-style pâté
(page 37)*

sauce over the hearts and serve immediately with creamed potato and carrots.

Prepare ahead. Cook the hearts, cool, cover and chill until required. Transfer the mixture to a large saucepan, bring to the boil stirring, cover and simmer for 20 minutes or until the hearts are heated through. Transfer to a serving plate and thicken the cooking liquid as above.

Note. Hearts are ideal for cooking in a slow cooker or crock-pot. Cook the hearts without the thickening for 8–10 hours on low or for 4–5 hours on high, adding the thickening 30 minutes before the end of the cooking time.

Serves 6.

Moussaka

METRIC/IMPERIAL
4 medium aubergines, sliced
salt and pepper
150 ml/¼ pint oil
2 medium onions, thinly sliced
2 garlic cloves, crushed
700 g/1½ lb lean minced lamb or half
    quantities each of lean minced lamb and
    lean minced beef
½ teaspoon dried oregano
½ teaspoon dried marjoram
¼ teaspoon ground cinnamon
2 tablespoons tomato purée
4 tomatoes, peeled and sliced
Sauce:
25 g/1 oz butter
25 g/1 oz flour
400 ml/¾ pint milk
¼ teaspoon dry mustard
salt and pepper
2 eggs, lightly beaten
AMERICAN
4 medium eggplant, sliced
salt and pepper
⅔ cup oil
2 medium onions, thinly sliced
2 garlic cloves, minced
1½ lb lean ground lamb, or half quantities
    each of lean ground lamb and lean
    ground beef
½ teaspoon dried oregano
½ teaspoon dried marjoram
¼ teaspoon ground cinnamon
2 tablespoons tomato paste
4 tomatoes, peeled and sliced
Sauce:
2 tablespoons butter
¼ cup flour
2 cups milk
¼ teaspoon dry mustard
salt and pepper
2 eggs, lightly beaten

Moussaka

Sprinkle the aubergine (eggplant) slices with salt and leave to drain in a colander for 30 minutes. Wash off the salt and dry with absorbent kitchen paper.

Meanwhile, heat a little of the oil in a large frying pan (skillet), add the onions and garlic and cook for 5 minutes or until soft. Add the meat, herbs, cinnamon and tomato purée (paste), season to taste and simmer gently for 10 minutes.

Heat some of the remaining oil and fry the aubergine (eggplant) slices a few at a time until golden brown. Transfer the slices to a plate as they brown. Use more oil as necessary.

Place a layer of aubergine (eggplant) slices in a shallow ovenproof dish. Cover with a layer of the meat mixture. Continue making layers until the ingredients are used up, finishing with a layer of aubergine (eggplant). Cover with the sliced tomatoes.

To make the sauce, melt the butter in a saucepan, add the flour and cook for 1 minute. Gradually stir in the milk and bring to the boil, stirring constantly. Stir in the mustard and seasoning to taste. Cook for 2 minutes. Pour a little of the sauce onto the eggs and stir well. Pour the egg mixture into the pan and stir well. Pour the sauce over the tomatoes.

Bake in a moderately hot oven, 190°C/375°F, Gas Mark 5 for 20 to 30 minutes or until bubbling and golden brown. Serve immediately with a green or tomato salad.

Prepare ahead. Pour the sauce over the tomatoes, cool, cover and chill in the refrigerator until required. Place the dish in a moderately hot oven and cook for 40 minutes or until bubbling and golden brown.

Curried Lamb Soup

METRIC/IMPERIAL
350 g/12 oz scrag end of neck of lamb
2 tablespoons oil
1 medium onion, chopped
1 garlic clove, crushed
750 ml/1¼ pints chicken stock
1 tablespoon curry powder
1 × 397 g/14 oz can tomatoes
salt and pepper
1 cooking apple, peeled, cored, chopped and
    mixed with the juice of ½ lemon
25 g/1 oz raisins
2 tablespoons chutney

AMERICAN
¾ lb boneless shoulder of lamb
2 tablespoons oil
1 medium onion, chopped
1 garlic clove, minced
3 cups chicken stock
1 tablespoon curry powder
1 × 14 oz can tomatoes
salt and pepper
1 cooking apple, peeled, cored, chopped and
    mixed with the juice of ½ lemon
3 tablespoons raisins
2 tablespoons chutney

Remove excess fat from the meat and cut into pieces. Heat the oil in a large saucepan, add the onion and garlic and cook, stirring, for 1 minute. Add the meat and turn in the mixture until lightly browned on all sides. Stir in the stock, bring the mixture to the boil and simmer for 1 hour or until the meat is very tender. Remove the meat from the pan. Reserve the meat and discard the bones.

Add the curry powder, tomatoes and the juice, seasoning to taste, apple and raisins to the stock mixture and bring to the boil, stirring. Cook quickly until the tomatoes have broken up and the liquid reduced slightly.

Add the reserved meat and the chutney, reduce the heat and simmer for 5 minutes or until heated through. Serve immediately with side dishes of rice, crispy fried noodles and sliced tomatoes to make a main dish.

Prepare ahead. Remove the pan from the heat after reducing the stock slightly. Stir in the meat and chutney, cool, pour into a container, cover and chill in the refrigerator until required. Reheat very gently until very hot. Serve as above.

Freeze. Add meat and chutney, pour into container, cover, label and freeze. Thaw in a saucepan, adding a little water if necessary, for about 1 hour until hot.

Beef 'n' bean casserole

METRIC/IMPERIAL
700 g/1½ lb lean minced beef
1 medium onion, chopped
1 × 219 g/8 oz can baked beans
1 × 226 g/8 oz can tomatoes
250 ml/8 fl oz beef stock
100 g/4 oz pasta whirls or shells
½ teaspoon dried thyme and marjoram
½ teaspoon chilli powder or 1 chilli, seeded
  and chopped, or to taste
1 teaspoon Worcestershire sauce
salt and pepper
chopped fresh parsley

AMERICAN
1½ lb lean ground beef
1 medium onion, chopped
1 × ½ lb can baked beans
1 × ½ lb can tomatoes
1 cup beef stock
1 cup pasta whirls or shells
½ teaspoon dried thyme or marjoram
½ teaspoon chili powder or 1 chili, seeded
  and chopped, or to taste
1 teaspoon Worcestershire sauce
salt and pepper
chopped fresh parsley

Mix together the beef, onion, baked beans, tomatoes and juice, stock, pasta, herbs, chilli to taste, Worcestershire sauce and salt and pepper to taste in a casserole. Stir the mixture so the ingredients are well mixed, cover and bake in a moderate oven, 160°C/325°F, Gas Mark 3 for 1½ hours or until the pasta is tender. When convenient stir the mixture occasionally to keep the pasta shapes from sticking together.

Serve the dish sprinkled with the parsley accompanied by green beans.
Prepare ahead. Cook the dish, cool, cover and chill in the refrigerator until required. Transfer the contents to a large saucepan and bring to the boil, stirring; if the mixture is dry add a little water. Cover the pan tightly and simmer for 15 minutes or until very hot. Transfer to a warmed casserole and serve immediately.

Left: Curried lamb soup

Right: Beef 'n' bean casserole

Beef in beer

METRIC/IMPERIAL

2 tablespoons vegetable oil
2 medium onions, sliced
4 celery stalks, roughly chopped
2 large carrots, sliced
*700 g/1½ lb chuck steak, trimmed of fat
    and cut into large chunks*
2 tablespoons flour
salt and pepper
400 ml/¾ pint light ale
2 thyme sprigs
1 bay leaf
¼ teaspoon dried marjoram
chopped fresh parsley to garnish

AMERICAN

2 tablespoons vegetable oil
2 medium onions, sliced
4 celery stalks, roughly chopped
2 large carrots, sliced
*1½ lb chuck steak, trimmed of fat and cut
    into large chunks*
2 tablespoons flour
salt and pepper
¾ pint beer
2 thyme sprigs
1 bay leaf
¼ teaspoon dried marjoram
chopped fresh parsley to garnish

Heat the oil in a frying pan (skillet). Add the onions, celery and carrots and cook gently for 5 minutes or until the onion is golden. Remove from the pan with a slotted spoon and place in a large casserole.

Roll the meat in the flour and season lightly. Fry the meat a few pieces at a time in the hot oil until lightly browned on all sides and transfer to the casserole as the pieces brown. Add more oil to the pan if necessary to fry the remaining meat. Stir any remaining flour into the sediment in the pan and gradually stir in the beer. Bring the mixture to the boil and pour into the casserole. Add the thyme, bay leaf and marjoram.

Cover the casserole and cook in a cool oven, 150°C/300°F, Gas Mark 2 for 2 to 2½ hours or until the meat is tender.

Discard the thyme and bay leaf, taste and adjust the seasoning if necessary, sprinkle with the parsley and serve with mashed potatoes or noodles.

Prepare ahead. When the meat is tender, cool, and chill in the refrigerator. To reheat, place the casserole in a moderately hot oven, 190°C/375°F, Gas Mark 5 and reheat for 30 minutes or until very hot. Alternatively, transfer the meat mixture to a saucepan. Bring to the

boil, stirring, reduce the heat to very low and simmer for 5 minutes. Pour into a warmed casserole and serve as above.
Freeze. Wrap, seal, label and freeze. Thaw in a moderately hot oven, 200°C/400°F, Gas Mark 6 for 1¼ hours or until bubbling.

Pork pie

METRIC/IMPERIAL

*500 g/1 lb skinned and boned pork, cut
    from shoulder, neck, spare ribs or lean
    end of belly*
*225 g/8 oz piece of bacon, rind and any
    bones removed*
salt and pepper
*1 teaspoon chopped fresh or ½ teaspoon
    dried sage*
¼ teaspoon ground mace
4 slices streaky bacon, rinds removed
Pastry:
450 g/1 lb flour
1 teaspoon salt
1 teaspoon icing sugar
150 ml/¼ pint water
100 g/4 oz lard, cut into pieces
*1 egg yolk beaten with 1 tablespoon water
    to glaze*
*300 ml/½ pint good homemade stock
    which sets when cold*

AMERICAN

1 lb boned pork
*½ lb piece of bacon, rind and any bones
    removed*
salt and pepper
*1 teaspoon chopped fresh or ½ teaspoon
    dried sage*
¼ teaspoon ground mace
4 bacon slices, rinds removed
Pastry:
4 cups flour
1 teaspoon salt
1 teaspoon confectioners' sugar
⅔ cup water
½ cup lard, cut into pieces
*1 egg yolk beaten with 1 tablespoon water
    to glaze*
*1¼ cups good homemade stock which sets
    when cold*

Cut the pork and bacon into small pieces. If liked, half the pork and half the bacon can be minced (ground). Fry the meat gently in its own fat until brown on all sides. Season the meat and stir in the sage and mace. Set aside to cool.

Meanwhile make the pastry; sift the flour, salt and sugar into a large bowl. Put the water in a saucepan and bring to the boil. Add the lard and, when melted,

pour slowly onto the flour mixture. Beat well until the mixture is smooth and comes away from the sides of the bowl. Leave to cool slightly.

Grease a 500 g/1 lb pie or loaf tin (pan). Roll out the dough on a floured surface and use two-thirds of it to line the tin (pan). Line the dough with the bacon slices. Place the pork mixture in the dough case and cover with the remaining dough. Pinch the edges together decoratively and make a large hole in the centre of the dough.

Bake the pie in a moderate oven, 160°C/325°F, Gas Mark 3 for 1½ to 2 hours or until the top is lightly browned and a skewer inserted in the hole through to the centre is hot to the touch when withdrawn. Remove the pie from the oven and leave to cool for 1 hour, then gently remove the pie from the tin (pan).

Brush the pastry with the beaten egg mixture, place on a baking sheet and return to the oven for 10 to 15 minutes to set the glaze. Cool the pie for 1 hour.

Heat the stock gently until just melted and pour through the hole in the centre of the pastry, using as much as the pie will hold. Leave the pie to cool completely.

Serve the pie cut into thick slices with a selection of salads.
Prepare ahead. Wrap the pie completely in aluminium foil and chill in the refrigerator until 30 minutes before required.
Freeze. Wrap, seal, label and freeze. Thaw in a moderately hot oven, 200°C/400°F, Gas Mark 6 for 30 minutes until crisp, remove and leave for 3 to 4 hours to finish thawing.

Polish meat loaf

METRIC/IMPERIAL

*1 kg/2 lb minced lean veal, or half
    quantities each of minced lean veal and
    minced lean beef*
1 medium onion, finely chopped
1 garlic clove, crushed
225 g/8 oz mushrooms, finely chopped
100 g/4 oz fresh white breadcrumbs
*75 ml/scant ⅛ pint dry white wine or
    stock*
1 egg, lightly beaten
salt and pepper
¼ teaspoon dried thyme
pinch of cayenne
150 ml/¼ pint soured cream
150 ml/¼ pint stock

Polish meat loaf: Pork pie

Illustrated overleaf: Golden harvest casserole

Garnish:
sliced tomatoes
sliced gherkins or dill pickles
AMERICAN
2 lb ground lean veal, or half quantities
    each of ground lean veal and ground
    lean beef
1 medium onion, finely chopped
1 garlic clove, minced
2 cups finely chopped mushrooms
2 cups fresh white breadcrumbs
⅓ cup dry white wine or stock
1 egg, lightly beaten
salt and pepper
¼ teaspoon dried thyme
pinch of cayenne
⅔ cup sour cream
⅔ cup stock
Garnish:
sliced tomatoes
sliced sweet-sour cucumbers

Put the meat in a large bowl with the onion, garlic, mushrooms and breadcrumbs and mix thoroughly. Add the wine or stock, egg, seasoning, thyme and cayenne and mix well to form a stiff mixture.

With wet hands shape the mixture into a loaf and place in a roasting pan. Pour over the sour(ed) cream and bake in a moderately hot oven, 200°C/400°F, Gas Mark 6 for 40 to 50 minutes or until the meat is cooked and a light crust has formed. Baste the loaf from time to time during cooking.

Transfer the meat to a serving dish. Place the roasting pan on top of the stove, pour in the stock and stir well to loosen any sediment, then boil until the stock is reduced by half. Strain this mixture over the meat and leave to cool. Garnish the meat with the tomatoes and gherkins or pickles (cucumbers) and serve with red cabbage salad.

Prepare ahead. When the meat is cooked transfer it to a large piece of aluminium foil and draw up the edges. Cool. Prepare the stock glaze as above and pour over the meat. Cover the meat completely with the foil and chill in the refrigerator until approximately 30 minutes before required.

Golden harvest casserole

METRIC/IMPERIAL
1 tablespoon clear honey
1 tablespoon cider vinegar
1 tablespoon soy sauce
150 ml/¼ pint dry cider
1 garlic clove, crushed
4 chicken joints
50 g/2 oz butter
2 medium onions, sliced
1 green pepper, seeded, cored and sliced
2 tablespoons flour
salt and pepper
1 × 425 g/15 oz can peach halves,
    drained
chopped fresh parsley to garnish
AMERICAN
1 tablespoon clear honey
1 tablespoon cider vinegar
1 tablespoon soy sauce
⅔ cup dry cider
1 garlic clove, minced
4 chicken joints
¼ cup butter
2 medium onions, sliced
1 green pepper, seeded, cored and sliced
2 tablespoons flour
salt and pepper
1 × 15 oz can peach halves, drained
chopped fresh parsley to garnish

Mix together the honey, vinegar, soy sauce, cider and garlic in a mixing bowl. Turn the chicken pieces in this mixture until well coated, cover the bowl and leave the chicken to marinate for 8 hours or overnight, turning occasionally. Drain the chicken and reserve the marinade.

Melt the butter in a large saucepan, add the chicken and brown on all sides. Remove the chicken. Add the onions to the pan and cook for 3 minutes. Add the pepper and cook for a further 4 minutes or until the onion is golden. Stir in the flour and cook for 1 minute.

Gradually stir in the reserved marinade and seasoning to taste. Bring the sauce to the boil, stirring, add the chicken pieces and simmer for 1 hour or until the chicken juices run clear when the thickest part is pierced with a skewer.

Place the peach halves in the pan and heat through for 5 minutes. Transfer the chicken pieces and peaches to a warmed serving dish and pour the sauce over. Sprinkle over the parsley and serve immediately.

Prepare ahead. Cook the chicken in the sauce but don't add the peaches. Transfer the chicken pieces and sauce to a container, cover and chill until required. Reheat the chicken pieces and sauce in a pan, stirring until hot, cover and simmer for 5 minutes. Add the peaches and heat for a further 5 minutes.

Midsummer lamb

METRIC/IMPERIAL
25 g/1 oz butter
1 medium onion, sliced
225 g/8 oz carrots, sliced
1 medium turnip, diced
500 g/1 lb boned leg or shoulder of lamb,
  cubed
100 g/4 oz button mushrooms, halved
150 ml/¼ pint dry cider
300 ml/½ pint stock
½ teaspoon dried oregano
salt and pepper
25 g/1 oz flour
2 tablespoons fresh single cream
AMERICAN
2 tablespoons butter
1 medium onion, sliced
1½ cups sliced carrots
1 medium turnip, diced
1 lb boned lamb, cubed
1 cup halved small mushrooms
⅔ cup hard cider
1¼ cups stock
½ teaspoon dried oregano
salt and pepper
¼ cup flour
2 tablespoons light cream

Melt the butter in a large saucepan, add the onion and cook for 5 minutes or until soft. Stir in the carrots and turnip and cook for a further 5 minutes or until the onion is golden. Stir in the meat and brown quickly on all sides. Add the mushrooms, cider, stock, oregano and salt and pepper to taste and bring to the boil. Cover and simmer for 1¼ hours or until the meat is cooked and tender. Pour a little of the cooking liquid into a bowl and stir in the flour to make a smooth paste. Stir into the cooking liquid and bring to the boil, stirring. Pour in the cream, stir quickly and transfer the mixture to a warmed serving dish. Serve immediately.

Prepare ahead. Cook the lamb, transfer to a container, cool, cover and chill until required. Remove any fat from the surface of the cooking liquid, put the mixture in a saucepan and reheat, stirring until hot. Mix in the flour and finish as above.

Golden harvest casserole (page 43): Midsummer lamb

Old fashioned steak and kidney casserole

METRIC/IMPERIAL
700 g/1½ lb chuck steak, cubed
175 g/6 oz ox kidney, cored and chopped
2 tablespoons flour
50 g/2 oz dripping
600 ml/1 pint beef stock
1 teaspoon dried mixed herbs
¼ teaspoon dried sage
salt and pepper
100 g/4 oz shelled mussels
AMERICAN
1½ lb chuck steak, cubed
6 oz beef kidney, cored and chopped
2 tablespoons flour
¼ cup beef drippings
2½ cups beef stock
1 teaspoon dried mixed herbs
¼ teaspoon dried sage
salt and pepper
¼ lb shucked mussels

Spread out the meat on a plate and sprinkle with the flour. Melt the dripping(s) and fry the meat quickly to brown on all sides. Place in a casserole as the meat browns. Stir any remaining flour into the pan and pour in the stock. Bring the mixture to the boil, stirring, add the herbs and season to taste. Pour into a casserole, cover and cook in a moderate oven, 160°C/325°F, Gas Mark 3 for 2 to 2½ hours or until the meat is very tender. When the meat is nearly cooked add the mussels and cook for a further 15 minutes or until heated through. Don't overcook or they will be tough.

Prepare ahead. Cook the meat until tender, don't add the mussels. Cool, cover and chill in the refrigerator until required. Remove any fat from the surface of the cooking liquid and reheat the casserole in a saucepan, stirring until hot. Add the mussels, cover and simmer for 15 minutes or until heated through. Transfer to a warmed serving dish.

Right: Old fashioned steak and kidney casserole

Beef olives

METRIC/IMPERIAL
1 kg/2 lb piece of beef (rump or skirt),
    thinly sliced
salt and pepper
100 g/4 oz fresh white breadcrumbs
2 medium onions, finely chopped
225 g/8 oz mushrooms, finely chopped
finely grated rind of 1 lemon
3 tablespoons chopped fresh parsley
½ teaspoon dried tarragon
1 egg, lightly beaten
2 tablespoons oil
25 g/1 oz flour
150 ml/¼ pint beef stock
1 garlic clove, crushed
1 tablespoon prepared French mustard
AMERICAN
2 lb very thinly sliced round steak or top
    round
salt and pepper
2 cups fresh white breadcrumbs
2 medium onions, finely chopped
2 cups finely chopped mushrooms
finely grated rind of 1 lemon
3 tablespoons chopped fresh parsley
½ teaspoon dried tarragon
1 egg, lightly beaten
2 tablespoons oil
¼ cup flour
⅔ cup beef stock
1 garlic clove, minced
1 tablespoon prepared French mustard

Dampen a board and a rolling pin and beat the meat until very thin. Season each slice of meat with salt and pepper to taste.

Mix together the breadcrumbs, onions, mushrooms, lemon rind, parsley and tarragon, then season lightly and bind with the egg. Divide the stuffing between the beef slices, roll up and secure with string.

Heat the oil in a frying pan (skillet) and quickly brown the beef olives on all sides. Transfer the beef olives to a casserole. Add the flour to the pan and cook for a few minutes until it starts to brown, stirring. Gradually stir in the stock, add the garlic and bring the mixture to the boil, stirring. Pour over the meat in the casserole, cover and cook in moderate oven, 160°C/325°F, Gas Mark 3 for 1¼ hours or until the meat is tender. Stir in the mustard, taste and adjust the seasoning if necessary, and serve immediately with boiled potatoes or rice and fresh vegetables.

Prepare ahead. When the meat is tender, add the mustard, cool the casserole, cover and chill in the refrigerator until required. Reheat in moderately hot oven 190°C/375°F, Gas Mark 5 for 30 minutes or until the tip of a knife inserted into the centre of an olive feels hot.

Freeze. Wrap, seal, label and freeze. Thaw in a saucepan for 40 to 50 minutes, adding a little water if necessary and turning the olives occasionally in the sauce, until hot.

Hungarian pork with sauerkraut

METRIC/IMPERIAL
1 tablespoon oil
500 g/1 lb onions, chopped
2 garlic cloves, crushed
700 g/1½ lb skinned and boned pork
    (belly, shoulder or spare rib), diced
700 g/1½ lb fresh sauerkraut
1 tablespoon paprika
1 red pepper, seeded, cored and chopped
1 tablespoon caraway seeds (optional)
500 g/1 lb tomatoes, peeled and roughly
    chopped
salt and pepper
25 g/1 oz flour
1 tablespoon water
150 ml/¼ pint soured cream
AMERICAN
1 tablespoon oil
1 lb onions, chopped
2 garlic cloves, minced
1½ lb boned pork, diced
1½ lb fresh sauerkraut
1 tablespoon sweet paprika
1 red pepper, seeded, cored and chopped
1 tablespoon caraway seeds (optional)
1 lb tomatoes, peeled and roughly chopped
salt and pepper
¼ cup flour
1 tablespoon water
⅔ cup sour cream

Heat the oil in a large saucepan, add the onions and garlic and cook for 7 minutes or until soft and golden. Increase the heat, add the meat and brown quickly on all sides. Add the sauerkraut, paprika, pepper, caraway seeds (if using) and the tomatoes. Stir well, season to taste, cover and simmer for 1½ hours or until the meat and sauerkraut are really tender.

Mix the flour to a smooth paste with the water and stir into the meat mixture. Cook for a further 5 minutes. Taste and adjust the seasoning if necessary. Pour the mixture into a warmed casserole, stir in the sour(ed) cream and serve immediately with black bread or mashed potatoes.

Prepare ahead. When the meat is tender, cool the mixture, pour into a container, cover and chill in the refrigerator. Transfer the mixture to a saucepan and reheat slowly, stirring occasionally. Add the flour and sour(ed) cream and serve as above.

Freeze. Do not add flour or sour(ed) cream. Wrap, seal, label and freeze. Thaw in a saucepan, reheating gently for about an hour, adding a little water if necessary. Finish as above.

Steak and kidney pie

700 g/1½ lb beef steak (rump, skirt or
    chuck), trimmed and cut into cubes
225 g/8 oz ox kidney, cored and cut into
    small pieces
50 g/2 oz flour
salt and pepper
50 g/2 oz butter
1 tablespoon oil
2 medium onions, roughly chopped
300 ml/½ pint beef stock
1 bay leaf
¼ teaspoon dried marjoram
¼ teaspoon dried sage
6–12 oysters, shelled with liquid reserved
    (optional)
1 tablespoon sherry
few drops Worcestershire sauce
Pastry:
50 g/2 oz butter
25 g/1 oz lard or shortening
100 g/4 oz flour
¼ teaspoon salt
75 ml/scant ⅛ pint cold water
beaten egg for brushing
AMERICAN
1½ lb beef steak (rump, round or chuck),
    trimmed and cut into cubes
½ lb beef kidney, cored and cut into pieces
½ cup flour
salt and pepper
¼ cup butter
1 tablespoon oil
2 medium onions, roughly chopped
1¼ cups beef stock
1 bay leaf
¼ teaspoon dried marjoram
¼ teaspoon dried sage
6–12 oysters, shucked with liquid
    reserved (optional)
1 tablespoon sherry
few drops Worcestershire sauce

Steak and kidney pie

Pastry:
¼ *cup butter*
2 tablespoons lard or shortening
1 cup flour
¼ *teaspoon salt*
⅓ *cup cold water*
beaten egg for brushing

Coat the steak and kidney in the flour seasoned with salt and pepper.

Heat the butter and oil in a frying pan (skillet). Add the onions and cook for 8 minutes or until golden. Transfer the onion to a casserole. Add the meat to the pan, a few pieces at a time, and brown quickly on all sides. As they brown transfer to the casserole. Sprinkle any remaining flour into the pan, cook for 1 minute, then gradually add the stock, stirring constantly, and stir in the bay leaf and herbs. Add the oysters and their liquid (if using), the sherry and Worcestershire sauce. Pour the mixture into the casserole and cook in a moderate oven, 160°C/325°F, Gas Mark 3 for 1½ hours or until the meat is tender. Discard the bay leaf. Taste and adjust the seasoning if necessary. Transfer to a 1 litre/2 pint/ 5 cup pie dish.

Meanwhile, make the pastry. Blend the butter and lard or shortening together and divide into 4 portions. Sift the flour and salt into a bowl and rub in one quarter of the fat. Mix to a firm dough with the water. Knead the dough lightly on a floured surface and roll out to a large rectangle.

Spread the rectangle with another quarter of the fat to within 2.5 cm/1 inch of the edges. Fold in three and press the edges to seal. Cover the dough and chill in the refrigerator for 15 minutes.

Roll out again into a rectangle and spread with the third quarter of the fat. Fold, seal and chill. Repeat the rolling, spreading and folding once more, using the last of the fat.

Roll out the dough until slightly larger than the rim of the pie dish. Cut off a strip and press it around the moistened rim of the dish. Moisten the dough strip and lay the remaining dough over the pie. Press the edges together and trim away the excess dough. Pinch the edges together. Make a hole in the centre and decorate the pie with dough leaves cut from the trimmings.

Brush the dough with beaten egg.

Bake the pie in a hot oven, 220°C/425°F, Gas Mark 7 for 30 minutes or until the pastry is golden brown and the sauce is bubbling.

Serve the pie immediately with a freshly cooked green vegetable.

Prepare ahead. Cover the pie with the dough but don't brush with beaten egg. Cover the dough carefully with plastic wrap or aluminium foil, then cover completely and chill in the refrigerator until needed. Brush the dough with beaten egg and bake the pie in a hot oven, 220°C/425°F, Gas Mark 7 for 30 minutes, reduce the heat to moderate, 180°C/350°F, Gas Mark 4 and cook for a further 10 minutes or until the filling is bubbling.

Freeze. Wrap, seal, label and freeze. Reheat from frozen as above allowing a further 40 minutes at the lower temperature to ensure that the filling is really hot.

Cassoulet

METRIC/IMPERIAL
175 g/6 oz butter beans, soaked overnight
 in cold water
40 g/1½ oz butter
225 g/8 oz breast of lamb, trimmed of fat
 and cut into strips
350 g/12 oz boned blade of pork, cubed
175 g/6 oz garlic-flavoured boiling
 sausage, sliced
100 g/4 oz salt pork or streaky bacon,
 chopped
2 medium onions, sliced
½ teaspoon dried mixed herbs
2 sprigs thyme
salt and pepper
600 ml/1 pint water

AMERICAN
1 cup butter beans, soaked overnight in
 cold water
3 tablespoons butter
½ lb breast of lamb, trimmed of fat and cut
 into strips
¾ lb boneless pork, cubed
6 oz garlic-flavoured boiling sausage,
 sliced
¼ lb salt pork or fatty bacon, chopped
2 medium onions, sliced
½ teaspoon dried mixed herbs
2 sprigs thyme
salt and pepper
2½ cups water

Cook the beans in boiling salted water for
20 minutes and drain.

Heat the butter in a large saucepan, add the lamb and pork and brown on all sides. Stir in the sausage and pork or bacon and cook, stirring, for 3 minutes. Stir in the onions, herbs, thyme, seasoning to taste, beans and water and bring the mixture to the boil, cover and simmer for 1½ to 2 hours or until all the meat and beans are cooked and very tender. Discard the thyme sprigs and serve very hot. **Prepare ahead.** Transfer to a container, cover, cool and chill in the refrigerator until required. Remove some of the fat from the surface before reheating in a large saucepan. Cover the pan tightly and simmer gently for 10 minutes until very hot.

Navarin of lamb

METRIC/IMPERIAL
2 breasts of lamb
25 g/1 oz flour
salt and pepper
25 g/1 oz lard
1 garlic clove, crushed
225 g/8 oz carrots, halved
1 × 397 g/14 oz can tomatoes
1 teaspoon dried mixed herbs
1 teaspoon grated lemon rind

AMERICAN
2 breasts of lamb
¼ cup flour
salt and pepper
2 tablespoons lard
1 garlic clove, minced
½ lb carrots, halved
1 × 14 oz can tomatoes
1 teaspoon dried mixed herbs
1 teaspoon grated lemon rind

Trim away excess fat from the meat and cut between the bones into portion-sized pieces. Coat the pieces in flour seasoned with salt and pepper and fry in the lard until lightly browned. As the pieces brown transfer them to a casserole. Stir in the garlic, carrots, tomatoes and the juice, herbs, lemon rind and seasoning to taste. Bring the mixture to the boil and pour into the casserole.

Cook the casserole in a moderate oven, 180°C/350°F, Gas Mark 4 for 1 to 1½ hours or until the meat is very tender and the sauce is thick. Serve very hot with boiled potatoes and broccoli.

Cassoulet

Prepare ahead. Cook the meat, cool, cover and chill the casserole until required. Remove any fat from the surface of the cooking liquid and bring to the boil in a saucepan. Simmer the mixture for 10 minutes or until very hot. Serve as above.

Freeze. When meat is tender, wrap, seal, label and freeze. Thaw in moderately hot oven, 200°C/400°F, Gas Mark 6 for 1¼ hours or until bubbling.

Carbonnade of beef

METRIC/IMPERIAL
700 g/1½ lb chuck steak, cubed
25 g/1 oz lard or dripping
1 medium onion, sliced
1 garlic clove, crushed
1 tablespoon flour
300 ml/½ pint brown ale
1 tablespoon lemon juice
salt and pepper
French bread cut into thick slices
French mustard

AMERICAN
1½ lb chuck steak, cubed
2 tablespoons lard or drippings
1 medium onion, sliced
1 garlic clove, minced
1 tablespoon flour
1¼ cups beer
1 tablespoon lemon juice
salt and pepper
French bread cut into thick slices
French mustard

Fry the meat in the lard or dripping(s) until the meat is lightly browned on all sides. Transfer the meat to a casserole. Add the onion and garlic to the pan and cook for 5 minutes. Stir in the flour, cook for 1 minute and gradually stir in the beer to make a smooth sauce.

Bring the mixture to the boil, stirring, and cook for 1 minute. Stir in the lemon juice and salt and pepper to taste. Pour over the meat, place the casserole in a moderate oven, 160°C/325°F, Gas Mark 3 and cook for 2 hours or until the meat is very tender.

Carbonnade of beef

Spread the French bread with the mustard and, 10 minutes before the end of cooking, remove the cover and place in the casserole. Serve the carbonnade very hot with peas and carrots.

Prepare ahead. Cook the meat until very tender, cover, cool and chill in the refrigerator until required. Transfer the mixture to a saucepan and bring to the boil, stirring. Pour into a warmed casserole, place the bread spread with mustard on top and heat through in a moderate oven, 180°C/350°F, Gas Mark 4 for 20 minutes.

Freeze. When meat is tender, wrap, seal, label and freeze. Thaw in moderately hot oven, 200°C/400°F, Gas Mark 6 for 1¼ hours or until bubbling. Add the bread and serve as above.

Bolognese sauce

METRIC/IMPERIAL

2 tablespoons vegetable oil
1 medium onion, finely chopped
1 garlic clove, crushed
100 g/4 oz bacon slices, rinds removed and chopped
2 celery stalks, finely chopped
1 medium carrot, grated
500 g/1 lb lean minced beef
2 tablespoons tomato purée
1 × 397 g/14 oz can tomatoes
300 ml/½ pint beef stock and 150 ml/¼ pint dry red wine or 450 ml/¾ pint stock
2 teaspoons chopped fresh or 1 teaspoon dried oregano or marjoram
½ teaspoon dried basil
1 teaspoon sugar
salt and pepper
25 g/1 oz grated Parmesan cheese

AMERICAN

2 tablespoons vegetable oil
1 medium onion, finely chopped
1 garlic clove, minced
½ cup chopped bacon
2 celery stalks, finely chopped
1 medium carrot, grated
1 lb lean ground beef
2 tablespoons tomato paste
1 × 14 oz can tomatoes
1¼ cups beef stock and ⅔ cup dry red wine or 2 cups stock
2 teaspoons chopped fresh or 1 teaspoon dried oregano or marjoram
½ teaspoon dried basil
1 teaspoon sugar
salt and pepper
¼ cup grated Parmesan cheese

Heat the oil in a saucepan, add the onion, garlic, chopped bacon, celery and grated carrot and fry for 5 minutes or until the onion is soft. Add the beef and cook gently until browned, breaking the meat up with a wooden spoon. Add the tomato purée (paste), tomatoes with the juice, stock and wine or stock, herbs, sugar and seasoning to taste. Bring to the boil, stirring, cover and simmer for 40 to 50 minutes, stirring occasionally, until the meat is cooked and the mixture is fairly thick. Stir in the cheese.

Serve the sauce with freshly cooked spaghetti or other pasta.

Prepare ahead. Make double the quantity, if liked, serve half with pasta as suggested above and use the other half to stuff cannelloni, or use in lasagne or moussaka. Assemble these dishes ahead of time in their cooking dishes, cover completely and chill in the refrigerator. Reheat in a moderately hot oven, 190°C/375°F, Gas Mark 5 for 30 to 40 minutes or until very hot and bubbling.

Freeze. Wrap, seal, label and freeze. Thaw from frozen in a saucepan with 2 tablespoons water, stirring occasionally, until very hot.

Country chicken and mushroom pie

METRIC/IMPERIAL

1½ kg/3 lb roasting chicken
2 medium onions
2 medium carrots, roughly chopped
6 black peppercorns
1 sprig rosemary
1 sprig thyme
½ bay leaf
½ teaspoon dried basil
salt and pepper
50 g/2 oz butter
225 g/8 oz button mushrooms, thinly sliced
25 g/1 oz flour
150 ml/¼ pint dry white wine or stock
4 tablespoons fresh single cream
225 g/8 oz frozen puff pastry, thawed
1 egg, beaten to glaze

AMERICAN

3 lb roasting chicken
2 medium onions
2 medium carrots, roughly chopped
6 black peppercorns
1 sprig rosemary
1 sprig thyme
½ bay leaf
½ teaspoon dried basil
salt and pepper
¼ cup butter
2 cups thinly sliced small mushrooms
¼ cup flour
⅔ cup dry white wine or stock
4 tablespoons light cream
½ lb frozen puff paste, thawed
1 egg, beaten to glaze

Put the chicken in a large saucepan. Cut one of the onions into quarters and add to the pan with the carrots, peppercorns, herbs and salt to taste. Barely cover the chicken with water and bring to the boil. Cover the pan and simmer gently for 1 hour or until the chicken juices run clear when the fat part of the thigh is pierced with a knife. Leave the chicken to cool in the cooking liquid. Remove chicken and strain and reserve the cooking liquid. Remove the chicken meat from the bones and cut into bite-sized pieces, discarding the skin.

Melt the butter in a frying pan (skillet). Chop the remaining onion, add to the pan and cook for 5 minutes or until soft. Add the mushrooms and fry for 2 minutes. Sprinkle in the flour and cook for 1 minute, stirring, then gradually stir in 150 ml/¼ pint/⅔ cup of the reserved cooking liquid and the white wine or stock. Bring to the boil, stirring, and simmer for 2 minutes. Remove the pan from the heat, stir in the cream and the chicken pieces. Pour the mixture into a 1 litre/2 pint/5 cup pie dish. Cool.

Roll out the pastry to an oblong slightly larger than the dish. Dampen the edge of the dish and cover with a strip cut from the pastry. Dampen the pastry strip and cover the pie with the remaining pastry. Press the edges together, trim away any excess pastry and pinch edges decoratively. Decorate the pie, if liked, with leaves cut from the trimmings.

Brush the pastry with the egg and bake in a moderately hot oven, 200°C/400°F, Gas Mark 6 for 30 to 40 minutes or until golden brown.

Serve immediately with peas and carrots or cabbage.

Prepare ahead. Pour the chicken mixture into the pie dish, cover completely, cool and chill in the refrigerator until required. Roll out the thawed pastry, cover the pie and cook as above.

Freeze. Transfer filling to an aluminium foil pie dish, wrap, seal, label and freeze. Thaw in the refrigerator for 12 hours. Cover with thawed pastry and continue as above.

Beef goulash

METRIC/IMPERIAL

25 g/1 oz beef dripping or 2 tablespoons oil
1 large onion, finely chopped
1 medium carrot, finely chopped
700 g/1½ lb chuck steak, trimmed of fat and cut into chunks
1 tablespoon flour
salt and pepper
1 teaspoon caraway seeds
1 tablespoon paprika
500 g/1 lb tomatoes, peeled, seeded and chopped
400 ml/¾ pint beef stock
2 tablespoons tomato purée
500 g/1 lb potatoes, diced
Garnish:
150 ml/¼ pint cultured soured cream
chopped fresh parsley

Beef goulash

AMERICAN

2 tablespoons oil
1 large onion, finely chopped
1 medium carrot, finely chopped
1½ lb chuck steak, trimmed of fat and cut
   into chunks
1 tablespoon flour
salt and pepper
1 teaspoon caraway seeds
1 tablespoon sweet paprika
1 lb tomatoes, peeled, seeded and chopped
2 cups beef stock
2 tablespoons tomato paste
1 lb potatoes, diced
Garnish:
⅔ cup sour cream
chopped fresh parsley

Heat the fat in a large saucepan, add the onion and fry for 3 minutes. Add the carrot and cook for a further 3 minutes or until the onion is golden. Roll the meat in the flour seasoned with salt and pepper. Remove the onion and carrot and set aside. Add the meat to the pan, a few pieces at a time, and brown quickly on all sides. Remove the meat as it browns, adding more fat to the pan if necessary.

Stir any remaining flour into the pan, add the caraway seeds and paprika and cook for 1 minute. Stir in the tomatoes, stock and purée (paste). Bring to the boil, stirring, return the meat and the vegetables to the pan and simmer very gently for 1½ hours. Alternatively, transfer the mixture to a casserole and cook in a cool oven, 150°C/300°F, Gas Mark 2 for 1½ hours. Stir in the diced potatoes and, whether cooking on top of the stove or in the oven, cook for a further hour or until the meat and potatoes are tender. Check the mixture occasionally, if it is too dry add a little water.

Transfer the goulash to a serving dish, if necessary. Stir the sour(ed) cream into the goulash and sprinkle with the parsley. The cream may be served separately, if preferred.

Serve this dish with a green vegetable or a mixed pepper salad and extra potatoes.

Prepare ahead. Cool the goulash, don't add the sour(ed) cream, transfer to a container if necessary and chill in the refrigerator until needed. Reheat in a saucepan, over low heat, stirring frequently until hot or in a casserole in a moderately hot oven, 190°C/375°F, Gas Mark 5 for 45 minutes or until bubbling. Serve as above.

Freeze. When cooked wrap, seal, label and freeze. Thaw in covered casserole in a moderately hot oven, 200°C/400°F, Gas Mark 6 for 1¼ hours or until bubbling. Stir in the sour(ed) cream and serve as above.

51

Lamb and bean hotpot

METRIC/IMPERIAL
100 g/4 oz haricot beans, soaked
   overnight in cold water
100 g/4 oz red kidney beans, soaked
   overnight in cold water
2 tablespoons oil
1 kg/2 lb neck of lamb, trimmed of fat
1 medium onion, sliced
salt and pepper
1 teaspoon dried mixed herbs
450 ml/¾ pint beef stock

AMERICAN
½ cup navy beans, soaked overnight in cold
   water
⅓ cup red kidney beans, soaked overnight
   in cold water
2 tablespoons oil
2 lb neck of lamb, trimmed of fat
1 medium onion, sliced
salt and pepper
1 teaspoon dried mixed herbs
2 cups beef stock

Boil the haricot (navy) and kidney beans
for 30 minutes and drain.

   Heat the oil in a large saucepan, add
the meat and brown well on all sides.
Add the onion and cook, stirring, for 3
minutes. Add salt and pepper to taste,
with the herbs and the stock and bring to
the boil. Add the par-cooked beans, cover
and simmer for 1½ hours or until the
meat and beans are tender and the
mixture fairly dry. Transfer to a warmed
dish and serve immediately.

Prepare ahead. Cook the hotpot, cover,
cool and chill in the refrigerator until
required. Remove any fat from the surface of the cooking liquid before reheating.

Lamb and bean hotpot

Tomato and beef cobbler

METRIC/IMPERIAL
25 g/1 oz butter
1 medium onion, chopped
100 g/4 oz mushrooms, chopped
500 g/1 lb lean minced beef
25 g/1 oz flour
300 ml/½ pint beef stock
1 × 397 g/14 oz can tomatoes
1 tablespoon tomato purée
1 teaspoon dried mixed herbs
½ teaspoon dried or fresh thyme
salt and pepper
Topping:
225 g/8 oz self-raising flour
½ teaspoon salt
½ teaspoon dry mustard
50 g/2 oz butter or margarine, cut into
    small pieces
150 ml/¼ pint milk
75 g/3 oz Cheddar cheese, grated
milk to glaze
AMERICAN
2 tablespoons butter
1 medium onion, chopped
1 cup chopped mushrooms
1 lb lean ground beef
¼ cup flour
1¼ cups beef stock
1 × 14 oz can tomatoes
1 tablespoon tomato paste
1 teaspoon dried mixed herbs
½ teaspoon dried or fresh thyme
salt and pepper
Topping:
2 cups flour sifted with 2 teaspoons
    baking powder
½ teaspoon salt
½ teaspoon dry mustard
¼ cup butter or margarine, cut into small
    pieces
⅔ cup milk
¾ cup grated Cheddar cheese
milk to glaze

Tomato and beef cobbler

Melt the butter in a large saucepan, add the onion and cook for 5 minutes or until soft. Add the mushrooms, cook for 1 minute, stir in the beef and cook, stirring, until browned and broken up. Sprinkle in the flour and gradually stir in the stock and tomatoes with the juice. Bring the mixture to the boil, stir in the purée (paste), herbs and salt and pepper to taste. Cover and simmer for 15 minutes.

Meanwhile, sift the flour, salt and mustard into a mixing bowl. Add the butter or margarine and rub in until the mixture resembles breadcrumbs. Stir in the milk to make a soft but not sticky dough. Roll or press out the dough to an oblong 1 cm/½ inch thick, sprinkle over the cheese and roll up. Cut into 14 pieces.

Pour the meat mixture into an oven-proof dish and arrange the dough circles, overlapping, on top. Brush with a little milk and bake in a moderately hot oven, 200°C/400°F, Gas Mark 6 for 30 minutes or until the topping is golden brown and the meat mixture bubbling. Serve immediately with Brussels sprouts and carrots.

Prepare ahead. Cook the meat mixture and place in the ovenproof dish. Cover and chill in the refrigerator until required. Rub the butter or margarine into the flour mixture, place in a polythene (plastic) bag and chill until required. Add the liquid just before using.

Biryani

METRIC/IMPERIAL

4 tablespoons oil
3 medium onions, sliced
2 lb lean lamb, cubed
4 garlic cloves, crushed
2.5 cm/1 inch piece fresh root ginger, peeled and chopped
1 teaspoon ground coriander
1 teaspoon ground cumin
½ teaspoon ground cinnamon
½ teaspoon ground cardamom
¼ teaspoon ground cloves
¼ teaspoon chilli powder
¼ teaspoon black pepper
300 ml/½ pint unsweetened yogurt
150 ml/¼ pint water
350 g/12 oz Basmati rice
salt
½ teaspoon powdered saffron, mixed with 2 tablespoons boiling water
25 g/1 oz butter
25 g/1 oz cashew nuts
25 g/1 oz blanched almonds
50 g/2 oz sultanas

AMERICAN

4 tablespoons oil
3 medium onions, sliced
2 lb boned lamb, cubed
4 garlic cloves, minced
1 inch piece fresh root ginger, peeled and chopped
1 teaspoon ground coriander
1 teaspoon ground cumin
½ teaspoon ground cinnamon
½ teaspoon ground cardamom
¼ teaspoon ground cloves
¼ teaspoon chili powder
¼ teaspoon black pepper
1¼ cups unsweetened yogurt
⅔ cup water
1¾ cups Basmati rice
salt
½ teaspoon powdered saffron, mixed with 2 tablespoons boiling water
2 tablespoons butter
¼ cup cashew nuts
¼ cup blanched almonds
⅓ cup golden raisins

Biryani

Heat the oil in a large saucepan, add the onion and cook until soft. Drain the onion and set aside. Add the meat to the pan and cook quickly until lightly browned on all sides. Add the garlic, ginger and spices and fry for 1 minute, stirring. Stir in the yogurt and water, reduce the heat to low and simmer for 30 to 40 minutes or until the meat is almost tender.

Cook the rice in boiling salted water for 5 minutes and drain well. Place the meat mixture, rice and onions in layers in a deep casserole and pour over the saffron water. Cover and cook in a moderate oven, 180°C/350°F, Gas Mark 4 for 30 minutes or until the rice and meat are tender.

Heat the butter in a frying pan (skillet) and fry the nuts until golden brown. Add the sultanas (raisins) and heat through. Pile the Biryani onto a serving dish and scatter the nuts and sultanas (raisins) over the top. Serve immediately with cucumber and yogurt, and poppadums. **Prepare ahead.** Place the meat mixture, rice and onions in layers in a casserole. Cover with aluminium foil and store in the refrigerator until required. Reheat in a moderately hot oven, 190°C/375°F, Gas Mark 5 for 30 minutes or until very hot. Serve with the nuts and sultanas (raisins) as above.

Serves 6.

Desserts

Preparing delicious main meals in advance shows you are practical, preparing desserts ahead of time shows you are resourceful! To help you in your enterprise, here is an irresistible selection of sweet dishes, which includes favourites and some which will be new to you. Most are suitable for rounding off family meals, all are ideal for entertaining and only a few are extravagant.

You will see that the pastry dishes are prepared up to the point of baking, wrapped tightly to prevent drying out and chilled until required. This gives lovely crisp pastry and is far more satisfactory than reheating the cooked dish. Of course, they can alternatively be cooked and served immediately.

If you want to serve a cold dessert soon after preparing, make sure you allow necessary time for setting or chilling. All chilled desserts, including soufflés, should be removed from the refrigerator for 15 to 30 minutes depending on the dish, before serving. This allows the sweet to develop its flavour and ensures the correct texture on serving.

Baked cheesecake

METRIC/IMPERIAL
225 g/8 oz digestive biscuits, finely crushed
50 g/2 oz butter, melted
500 g/1 lb cream cheese, softened
2 tablespoons thick honey
50 g/2 oz brown sugar
¼ teaspoon mixed spice
¼ teaspoon salt
2 eggs, beaten

AMERICAN
½ lb digestive biscuits or Graham crackers, finely crushed
¼ cup butter, melted
2 × 8 oz packages cream cheese, softened
2 tablespoons thick honey
⅓ cup brown sugar
¼ teaspoon mixed spice
¼ teaspoon salt
2 eggs, beaten

Put the biscuits (crackers) in a bowl and stir in the melted butter, mixing until thoroughly combined. Using a metal spoon, press the crumb mixture into the base and sides of a buttered 18 cm/7 inch loose-bottomed cake tin (springform pan). Chill in the refrigerator for 30 minutes or until quite firm.

Meanwhile, prepare the filling. Blend the cheese, honey, sugar, spice and salt together in a bowl, then beat in the eggs, one at a time, until light and creamy. Pour the filling into the crumb case and bake in a cool oven, 150°C/300°F, Gas Mark 2 for 45 to 55 minutes or until the filling is set. Turn off the oven and leave the cheesecake to cool in the oven. When cold, lift onto a plate on the loose bottom and serve cut into wedges.

Prepare ahead. When the cheesecake is cold, cover the top of the tin closely with plastic wrap or aluminium foil and chill in the refrigerator until 15 minutes before required.

Freeze. Open freeze, wrap, seal, label and freeze. Thaw overnight in refrigerator or for 4 to 5 hours at room temperature.

Serves 6–8.

Crêpes Suzette

METRIC/IMPERIAL
100 g/4 oz flour
¼ teaspoon salt
2 eggs, beaten
300 ml/½ pint milk
oil for frying
Sauce:
100 g/4 oz caster sugar
finely grated rind and juice of 2 oranges
2 tablespoons brandy
2 tablespoons orange-flavoured liqueur
AMERICAN
1 cup flour
¼ teaspoon salt
2 eggs, beaten
1¼ cups milk
oil for frying
Sauce:
½ cup sugar
finely grated rind and juice of 2 oranges
2 tablespoons brandy
2 tablespoons orange-flavored liqueur

Sift the flour and salt into a bowl. Make a well in the centre, add the eggs then gradually add half the milk. Beat vigorously with a wooden spoon until the batter is completely smooth. Stir in the remaining milk. Heat a little oil in a small frying pan (skillet) until very hot, but not smoking. Pour a little of the batter, about 2 tablespoons, into the pan tilting it quickly to cover the base with the batter. Cook quickly until the underneath is golden brown, turn over the pancake (crêpe) and quickly cook the other side until golden. Slide out the pancake (crêpe) and keep warm. Use the remaining batter to make 10 or 12 pancakes (crêpes).

Heat the sugar in a large frying pan (skillet) and cook over low heat until pale golden. Stir in the orange rind and juice with a wooden spoon, fold the crêpes and slide them into the sauce. Pour over the brandy and liqueur, heat for 1 minute and ignite, if wished. Serve immediately.
Prepare ahead. Cook the pancakes (crêpes) and slide them onto a wire rack to cool. Make a pile of them, placing a square of oiled greaseproof (waxed) paper between each to prevent them sticking together and wrap the pile completely in aluminium foil. Chill the pancakes in the refrigerator until required. Make the sauce and reheat the pancakes (crêpes) in the sauce before pouring over the spirits and serving as above.
Freeze. Cooked pancakes freeze well: stack them, interleaving each one with

56

Left: Yorkshire apple tart

oiled greaseproof (waxed) paper, wrap, seal, label and freeze. Thaw, spread out individually, for 20 to 30 minutes at room temperature. Reheat pancakes in a little oil or butter for 30 seconds on each side.

Yorkshire apple tart

METRIC/IMPERIAL
275 g/10 oz plain flour
½ teaspoon salt
65 g/2½ oz shortening, cut into small pieces
65 g/2½ oz margarine or butter, cut into small pieces
about 2 tablespoons water
350 g/12 oz cooking apples, peeled, cored and sliced
2 tablespoons sugar
¼ teaspoon dried sage
1 tablespoon water
100 g/4 oz Cheddar cheese, sliced
sugar for sprinkling
AMERICAN
2½ cups flour
½ teaspoon salt
⅓ cup shortening, cut into small pieces
⅓ cup margarine or butter, cut into small pieces
about 2 tablespoons water
¾ lb cooking apples, peeled, cored and sliced
2 tablespoons sugar
¼ teaspoon dried sage
1 tablespoon water
¼ lb Cheddar cheese, sliced
sugar for sprinkling

Sift the flour and salt into a mixing bowl. Add the shortening and margarine or butter and rub in until the mixture resembles fine breadcrumbs. Add enough water to make a stiff dough. Knead the dough lightly on a floured surface, roll out two-thirds of the dough to a large circle and line a 20 cm/8 inch flan tin (pan). Fill with apples and sprinkle over the sugar and sage. Add the water. Roll out the remaining pastry to a circle, trim the edges to make the circle the same size as the tin (pan) and pinch the edges decoratively. Lift the pastry and lay it over the filling, but don't press the edges together. If liked cut out shapes from the trimmings and decorate the top of the pie.

Upside-down toffee apple tart

Bake in a moderately hot oven, 200°C/400°F, Gas Mark 6 for 20 minutes or until the pastry is cooked but not coloured. Remove the tart from the oven, cool slightly and carefully remove the top. Arrange the cheese slices over the filling, replace the top and return to the oven for a further 10 to 15 minutes or until the pastry is golden brown.

Serve the tart hot or warm, sprinkled with sugar.

Prepare ahead. Prepare the tart but don't cook it. Cover completely in plastic wrap or aluminium foil and chill in the refrigerator until required. Remove wrappings and bake and serve as above.

Serves 4–6.

Upside-down toffee apple tart

METRIC/IMPERIAL
100 g/4 oz flour
¼ teaspoon salt
1 tablespoon icing sugar
50 g/2 oz butter, cut into small pieces
1 egg yolk, lightly beaten with ½ teaspoon vinegar
1 tablespoon cold water
Filling:
100 g/4 oz sugar
1 tablespoon water
25 g/1 oz butter
¼ teaspoon grated nutmeg
500 g/1 lb cooking or dessert apples
AMERICAN
1 cup flour
¼ teaspoon salt
1 tablespoon confectioners' sugar
¼ cup butter, cut into small pieces
1 egg yolk, lightly beaten with ½ teaspoon vinegar
1 tablespoon cold water

Filling:
½ cup sugar
1 tablespoon water
2 tablespoons butter
¼ teaspoon grated nutmeg
1 lb tart or cooking or dessert apples

Sift the flour, salt and sugar into a mixing bowl, add the butter and rub in until the mixture resembles fine breadcrumbs. Stir in the egg mixture and enough water to make a stiff dough. Cover the dough and chill in the refrigerator for 30 minutes.

Meanwhile, put the sugar, water, half the butter and the nutmeg in a small saucepan and heat gently until the mixture has melted and turned golden brown. Pour immediately into a buttered 23 cm/9 inch cake tin (pan) and tilt until the base of the tin (pan) is covered. Leave to set.

Peel and core the apples and cut into thin slices. Arrange the slices, overlapping, in circles on top of the toffee base. Dot with the remaining butter. Roll out the chilled dough to a circle large enough to cover the apple slices. Place it on top and seal the edges of the pastry to the lip of the tin (pan) with a little water. Prick the dough with a fork.

Bake the tart in a hot oven, 220°C/425°F, Gas Mark 7 for 30 minutes or until the pastry is pale golden brown. Cool for a few minutes, place a warm serving plate over the pastry and invert so that the tart slides onto the plate. Serve warm or cold with single (light) cream.

Prepare ahead. Prick the dough with a fork, cover completely with plastic wrap and chill in the refrigerator until required. Cook and serve as above.

Freeze. Prick the dough with a fork, wrap, seal, label and freeze. Thaw in a hot oven, 220°C/425°F, Gas Mark 7 for 40 to 50 minutes or until golden. Serve as above.

Blackberry and apple pie

METRIC/IMPERIAL

225 g/8 oz flour

½ teaspoon salt

50 g/2 oz shortening, cut into small
   pieces

50 g/2 oz butter or margarine, cut into
   small pieces

1 tablespoon caster sugar

2 tablespoons water

Filling:

225 g/8 oz blackberries

500 g/1 lb cooking apples, peeled, cored
   and sliced into water with 1 tablespoon
   lemon juice added

finely grated rind of ½ lemon

100 g/4 oz caster sugar, or to taste

15 g/½ oz butter

½ teaspoon ground cinnamon

AMERICAN

2 cups flour

½ teaspoon salt

¼ cup shortening, cut into small pieces

¼ cup butter or margarine, cut into small
   pieces

1 tablespoon sugar

2 tablespoons water

Filling:

½ lb blackberries

1 lb tart or cooking apples, peeled, cored
   and sliced into water with 1 tablespoon
   lemon juice added

finely grated rind of ½ lemon

½ cup sugar, or to taste

15 g/½ oz butter

½ teaspoon ground cinnamon

Sift the flour and salt into a mixing bowl,
add the fats and rub in until the mixture
resembles fine breadcrumbs. Stir in the
sugar and enough water to make a stiff
dough. On a lightly floured surface
knead the dough lightly. Divide the
dough in half and roll out half to a circle
large enough to cover a 20 cm/8 inch pie
dish (pan) or plate. Chill in the refrigerator while preparing the filling.

Place the blackberries in a large bowl.
Stir in the apples, together with the
lemon rind and sugar and mix well. Mix
together the butter and cinnamon.
Spoon the fruit mixture into the pastry
case and dot with small pieces of the
cinnamon butter. Roll out the remaining
dough to a circle and lay it over the
filling. Dampen the pastry edges, press
together to seal, trim and decorate them.
Make a small hole in the centre of the
pastry.

Bake in a moderately hot oven,
200°C/400°F, Gas Mark 6 for 40 minutes or until the pastry is golden brown
and the filling cooked. Reduce the oven
temperature to moderate if the pastry is
browning too much.

Serve immediately, or serve warm or
cold, with custard, cream or ice cream.

Prepare ahead. Complete the pie but
don't bake it. Cover completely with
aluminium foil and chill in the refrigerator until required. Bake and serve as
above.

Freeze. Open freeze, wrap, seal, label and
freeze. Thaw in a hot oven, 220°C/
425°F, Gas Mark 7 for 30 minutes. Make
a slit in the pie, cover with foil, reduce
heat to moderately hot, 190°C/375°F,
Gas Mark 5 and bake for a further 40
minutes or until apples are tender. Remove covering for last 10 minutes to
crisp pastry.

Serves 4–6.

Uncooked cheesecake

METRIC/IMPERIAL

50 g/2 oz butter

225 g/8 oz digestive biscuits, finely
   crushed

350 g/12 oz cream cheese, softened

75 g/3 oz caster sugar

2 eggs, separated

finely grated rind and juice of 1 lemon

15 g/½ oz powdered gelatine

3 tablespoons water

300 ml/½ pint fresh double cream, lightly
   whipped

50 g/2 oz plain chocolate, grated, to
   decorate

AMERICAN

¼ cup butter

½ lb digestive or Graham crackers, finely
   crushed

1½ cups cream cheese, softened

⅓ cup sugar

2 eggs, separated

finely grated rind and juice of 1 lemon

1 envelope unflavored gelatin

3 tablespoons water

1¼ cups heavy cream, lightly whipped

2 squares semi-sweet chocolate, grated, to
   decorate

Melt the butter in a saucepan and stir in
the biscuit (cracker) crumbs. Spoon into
a 25 cm/10 inch loose-bottom cake tin
(springform pan) and press evenly

against the base. Bake in a moderately
hot oven, 190°C/375°F, Gas Mark 5 for
10 minutes. Remove from the oven and
cool.

Beat the cream cheese with the sugar
and egg yolks until the mixture is light
and creamy. Stir in the lemon rind.
Sprinkle the gelatin(e) over the water in
a small bowl and leave for 5 minutes.
Place in a pan of hot water and heat
gently, stirring, until dissolved. Stir the
lemon juice and dissolved gelatin(e) into
the cheese mixture and beat well. Beat
the egg whites until stiff, fold into the
cheese mixture and then carefully fold in
the cream. Pour the mixture into the tin
(pan) and leave to set.

Lift the cheesecake onto a serving dish
on the loose bottom and serve sprinkled
with grated chocolate.

Prepare ahead. If pressed for time omit
the baking of the crumb case. Pour the
mixture into the crumb case. Cover the
tin closely with plastic wrap or aluminium foil and chill in the refrigerator
until 30 minutes before required.

Freeze. Open freeze, wrap, seal, label and
freeze. Thaw overnight in the refrigerator or for 4 to 5 hours at room
temperature.

Serves 4–6.

Chocolate mocha Bavarian cream

METRIC/IMPERIAL

4 eggs, separated

100 g/4 oz caster sugar

½ teaspoon cornflour

450 ml/¾ pint milk

75 g/3 oz plain chocolate, broken into
   pieces

15 g/½ oz gelatine

2 tablespoons strong black liquid coffee

2 tablespoons orange-flavoured liqueur
   (optional)

150 ml/¼ pint fresh double cream, lightly
   whipped

AMERICAN

4 eggs, separated

½ cup sugar

½ teaspoon cornstarch

2 cups milk

3 squares semi-sweet chocolate, broken
   into pieces

1 envelope unflavored gelatin

2 tablespoons strong black liquid coffee

2 tablespoons orange-flavored liqueur
   (optional)

⅔ cup heavy cream, lightly whipped

Strawberry mousse; Rhubarb suédoise (page 60); Iced honey and brandy mousse (page 60)

Beat the egg yolks with half the sugar and the cornflour (cornstarch) until light and creamy. Scald the milk, add the chocolate pieces and stir until melted. Pour slowly onto the egg mixture, stirring constantly, then return the mixture to the pan and heat gently until hot and slightly thickened, do not allow to boil. Cool slightly.

Sprinkle the gelatin(e) over the coffee in a small bowl and leave for 5 minutes. Place the bowl in a pan of hot water and heat gently, stirring, until the gelatin(e) has dissolved. Stir into the custard mixture. Stir in the liqueur (if using) and leave to cool, stirring occasionally.

Beat the egg whites until stiff, beat in the remaining sugar a spoonful at a time and fold into the custard. Carefully fold in the cream. Pour into a serving or soufflé dish or 6 individual dishes and leave in a cool place to set.

Prepare ahead. Pour into dishes, cover and chill in the refrigerator until 30 minutes before required.

Freeze. Wrap, seal, label and freeze. Thaw for 4 to 5 hours at room temperature in a large bowl, if in individual bowls allow 2 to 3 hours.

Serves 6.

Strawberry mousse

METRIC/IMPERIAL
500 g/1 lb strawberries
15 g/½ oz powdered gelatine
2 tablespoons water
juice of 1 lemon
150 g/5 oz caster sugar
2 egg whites
150 ml/¼ pint fresh double cream, lightly whipped
Decoration:
150 ml/¼ pint fresh double cream
5 whole strawberries
AMERICAN
1 lb strawberries
1 envelope unflavored gelatin
2 tablespoons water
juice of 1 lemon
⅔ cup sugar
2 egg whites
⅔ cup heavy cream, lightly whipped
Decoration:
⅔ cup heavy cream
5 whole strawberries

Prepare a 600 ml/1 pint/2½ cup soufflé dish: cut a strip of doubled greaseproof (waxed) paper long enough to go around the outside of the dish and overlap by 2.5 cm/1 inch and be 5 cm/2 inches higher than the dish. Tie this securely around the outside of the dish. Brush the inside of the paper above the rim with a little melted butter.

Purée the strawberries in an electric blender or rub them through a nylon sieve into a bowl. Sprinkle the gelatin(e) over the water in a small bowl and leave for 5 minutes. Stand the bowl in a saucepan of hot water, place over low heat and stir until dissolved. Add the lemon juice and sugar and stir until the sugar has dissolved. Stir gelatin(e) mixture into the strawberry purée and taste for sweetness – the mixture should be a little oversweet at this point. Leave to cool and thicken a little.

Beat the egg whites until stiff, fold into the strawberry mixture and fold in the whipped cream. Spoon into the soufflé dish and chill in the refrigerator until set. Remove the paper collar carefully and decorate the soufflé with whipped cream and whole strawberries.

Prepare ahead. Chill the soufflé until set, carefully cover the dish and soufflé with aluminium foil and chill in the refrigerator until 1 hour before required. Decorate as above.

Freeze. Open freeze, wrap, seal, label and freeze. Thaw for 4 to 5 hours at room temperature.

Iced honey and brandy mousse

METRIC/IMPERIAL
3 eggs, separated
2 tablespoons clear honey
2 tablespoons lemon juice
2 tablespoons orange juice
2 tablespoons brandy
150 ml/¼ pint fresh double cream, lightly whipped
fan wafers to serve
AMERICAN
3 eggs, separated
2 tablespoons clear honey
2 tablespoons lemon juice
2 tablespoons orange juice
2 tablespoons brandy
⅔ cup heavy cream, lightly whipped
fan wafers to serve

Beat the egg yolks, honey, lemon and orange juice, and brandy together with an electric beater until the mixture is thick and light and has almost doubled in volume. In a clean bowl, beat the egg whites until stiff, then fold into the egg yolk mixture. Fold in the cream and pour into a 600 ml/1 pint/2½ cup soufflé or glass dish or 6 individual dishes. Chill in the frozen food storage compartment until set and slightly frozen. Serve slightly frozen with the fan wafers.

Prepare ahead. Pour the mixture into the dishes, cover with plastic wrap and chill in the frozen food storage compartment until required. If you prefer the mousse to be softer, remove from the compartment and place in the body of the refrigerator 30 minutes before required.

Freeze. Open freeze, wrap, seal, label and freeze. If liked instead of thawing for 1 to 2 hours, serve the mousse frozen.

 Serves 6.

Lemon soufflé

METRIC/IMPERIAL
finely grated rind of 2 lemons
4 tablespoons lemon juice
3 eggs, separated
75 g/3 oz sugar
1 tablespoon powdered gelatine
4 tablespoons water
300 ml/½ pint fresh double cream
Decoration:
150 ml/¼ pint fresh double cream
about 12 ratafia biscuits

60

AMERICAN
finely grated rind of 2 lemons
4 tablespoons lemon juice
3 eggs, separated
6 tablespoons sugar
1 envelope unflavored gelatin
4 tablespoons water
1¼ cups heavy cream
Decoration:
⅔ cup heavy cream
about 12 Graham crackers

Prepare a 600 ml/1 pint/2½ cup soufflé dish: cut a strip of doubled greaseproof (waxed) paper long enough to go around the outside of the dish and overlap by 2.5 cm/1 inch and to be 5 cm/2 inches higher than the dish. Tie this securely around the outside of the dish with string. Brush the inside of the paper above the rim very lightly with melted butter.

 Put the lemon rind and juice, egg yolks and sugar in a large mixing bowl and stand over a pan of hot water. Beat the mixture with a rotary beater or whisk until thick.

 Sprinkle the gelatin(e) over the water in a small bowl. Leave for 5 minutes, then place the bowl in a pan of hot water and stir over low heat until the gelatin(e) has dissolved. Cool slightly, stir into the lemon mixture and leave until half set.

 Whip the cream until thick, then fold into the lemon mixture. Beat the egg whites until stiff and fold into the lemon mixture. Spoon into the prepared soufflé dish and chill in the refrigerator for at least 2 hours or until set.

 Remove the paper collar carefully. Crush some of the ratafias (Graham crackers) and press onto the sides of the soufflé. Decorate the top with piped whipped cream and whole ratafias or other decorative biscuits (cookies).

Prepare ahead. Chill the soufflé until set. Carefully cover the dish and soufflé with aluminium foil and chill in the refrigerator until 1 hour before required. Decorate as above.

Freeze. Open freeze, wrap, seal, label and freeze. Thaw for 4 to 5 hours at room temperature. Serves 4–6.

Rhubarb suédoise

METRIC/IMPERIAL
500 g/1 lb rhubarb, cut into 2.5 cm/ 1 inch lengths
225 g/8 oz sugar
25 g/1 oz cornflour
2 tablespoons water
1 tablespoon caster sugar
AMERICAN
1 lb rhubarb, cut into 1 inch lengths
1 cup sugar
2 tablespoons cornstarch
2 tablespoons water
1 tablespoon sugar

Put the rhubarb in a bowl, cover with the sugar and leave for at least 1 hour to draw out the juice. Put the rhubarb and juice in a saucepan, add as much water as is needed just to cover the rhubarb and bring to the boil. Cover and simmer for 20 to 30 minutes or until the rhubarb is very soft and has almost disintegrated.

 Mix the cornflour (cornstarch) to a smooth paste with the water. Pour onto the rhubarb and, stirring, boil the mixture for 3 minutes or until the cloudiness disappears and the mixture thickens. Taste for sweetness, adding more sugar if necessary. Rinse a mould or bowl with water, then pour in the rhubarb and leave until set. Turn out the suédoise onto a chilled plate and sprinkle over the sugar just before serving.

Prepare ahead. Pour the rhubarb mixture into the mould or bowl, cover and chill in the refrigerator until 15 minutes before required. Turn out and sprinkle with the sugar. For a special occasion decorate the mould with whipped cream and baby meringues.

Freeze. Wrap, seal, label and freeze. Thaw for 4 to 5 hours at room temperature.

Gooseberry fool

METRIC/IMPERIAL
500 g/1 lb gooseberries, washed but not topped and tailed
5 tablespoons water
100 g/4 oz sugar
300 ml/½ pint milk or fresh single cream
2 egg yolks
1 teaspoon cornflour
150 ml/¼ pint fresh double cream, lightly whipped
sponge fingers to serve

AMERICAN
1 lb gooseberries, washed but not trimmed
⅓ cup water
½ cup sugar
1¼ cups milk or light cream
2 egg yolks
1 teaspoon cornstarch
⅔ cup heavy cream, lightly whipped
ladyfingers to serve

Put the gooseberries in a saucepan with the water and sugar. Poach the fruit very gently until soft and then rub through a nylon sieve into a bowl. Cool.

Meanwhile, heat the milk or cream to just below boiling point. Beat the egg yolks and cornflour (cornstarch) together in a bowl and pour in the milk or cream. Place the bowl over a pan of simmering water and stir until the custard thickens enough to coat the back of the spoon. Cool. Mix the gooseberry purée into the custard and taste for sweetness, adding more sugar if necessary. Leave until cold. Fold in the cream.

Cover the mixture and chill in the refrigerator until 30 minutes before required. Spoon the mixture into 4 individual dishes or glasses and serve with the sponge (lady) fingers.
Freeze. Wrap, seal, label and freeze. Thaw for 3 to 4 hours at room temperature.

Raspberry soufflé

METRIC/IMPERIAL
500 g/1 lb raspberries
4 egg whites
225 g/8 oz caster sugar
300 ml/½ pint fresh double cream, lightly
    whipped
Decoration:
150 ml/¼ pint fresh double cream
few whole raspberries
AMERICAN
3 cups raspberries
4 egg whites
1 cup sugar
1¼ cups heavy cream, lightly whipped
Decoration:
⅔ cup heavy cream
few whole raspberries

Purée the raspberries in an electric blender or rub them through a nylon sieve. Beat the egg whites until stiff, then slowly beat in the sugar, a spoonful at a time. Fold in the raspberry purée, then fold in the whipped cream. Pour the mixture into a soufflé dish. Cover the dish and chill in the refrigerator until 30 minutes before required.

Whip the cream until it forms soft peaks. Spoon the cream into a piping bag fitted with a fluted nozzle and pipe it decoratively in swirls. Alternatively spoon the cream on top. Decorate each swirl with a raspberry.
Freeze. Open freeze, wrap, seal, label and freeze. Thaw for 1 hour at room temperature if serving iced, leave for 3 to 4 hours to thaw completely.

Serves 4–6.

Lemon soufflé; Gooseberry fool; Raspberry soufflé

Chocolate mousse

METRIC/IMPERIAL
225 g/8 oz plain chocolate, broken into
  pieces
2 tablespoons water
4 eggs, separated
1 tablespoon rum (optional)
Decoration:
150 ml/¼ pint fresh double cream
1 small chocolate flake, crumbled
AMERICAN
8 squares semi-sweet chocolate, broken
  into pieces
2 tablespoons water
4 eggs, separated
1 tablespoon rum (optional)
Decoration:
⅔ cup heavy cream
2 squares semi-sweet chocolate,
  grated

Put the chocolate pieces and water in a small bowl and stand in a pan of hot water. Heat gently until the chocolate melts. Don't let the chocolate get too hot. Cool slightly. Stir the egg yolks into the melted chocolate, one at a time, then stir in the rum (if using).

Beat the egg whites until stiff. Spoon the chocolate mixture into the bowl and carefully fold in the egg whites until just mixed.

Spoon the mixture into a dish or 4 individual dishes and leave in a cool place until set. Whip the cream and decorate the mousse. Sprinkle with the chocolate and serve.

Prepare ahead. Pour into dishes, cover and chill in the refrigerator until 30 minutes before required. Decorate as above just before serving.

Freeze. Wrap, seal, label and freeze. Thaw for 2 to 3 hours in the refrigerator.

Pears in red wine

METRIC/IMPERIAL
225 g/8 oz sugar
5 cm/2 inch piece of cinnamon stick
2.5 cm/1 inch piece fresh root ginger
2 cloves
4 strips orange peel
2 strips lemon peel
400 ml/14 fl oz red wine
6 firm pears
2 teaspoons arrowroot
AMERICAN
1 cup sugar
2 inch piece of cinnamon stick
1 inch piece fresh root ginger
2 cloves
4 strips orange peel
2 strips lemon peel
1¾ cups red wine
6 firm pears
2 teaspoons arrowroot

Put the sugar, cinnamon, ginger, cloves, peel and wine in a large saucepan and bring slowly to the boil, stirring until the sugar has dissolved. Boil for 1 minute. Peel the pears, leaving the stalks on and removing the flower from the other end. Place the pears in the syrup, cover the pan and poach the pears for about 30 minutes or until tender.

Remove the pears from the pan. Strain the syrup into a measuring jug, reduce the syrup to 300 ml/½ pint/1¼ cups, if necessary.

Mix the arrowroot with a little water to a smooth paste and stir into the syrup. Bring to the boil and simmer for 1 minute or until the mixture clears and thickens slightly. Arrange the pears on a serving dish and pour over the syrup to coat them. Leave until completely cold and serve with cream.

Prepare ahead. Put the cooked pears in a container and pour over the thickened sauce. Cover and chill in the refrigerator until required. Transfer to a serving dish and serve as above.

Freeze. Wrap, seal, label and freeze. Thaw for 5 to 6 hours at room temperature. Serves 6.

Pears in red wine

Apple and chocolate crunch pudding

METRIC/IMPERIAL
75 g/3 oz butter
1 × 300 g/10½ oz packet chocolate digestive biscuits, crushed
3 medium cooking apples, peeled and sliced
grated rind and juice of 1 orange
2 tablespoons golden syrup
AMERICAN
⅓ cup butter
1 × 10½ oz package chocolate covered cookies, crushed
3 medium cooking apples, peeled and sliced
grated rind and juice of 1 orange
2 tablespoons light corn syrup

Melt the butter in a saucepan, add the biscuits (cookies) and stir until coated with the butter. Remove from the heat.

Grease an ovenproof dish well with butter and put in half the apple slices, sprinkle over half the rind and pour over half the juice and half the syrup. Repeat the layers. Cover the dish lightly and bake in a moderately hot oven, 190°C/375°F, Gas Mark 5 for 30 minutes or until the apples are tender. Serve hot or cold with cream.

Prepare ahead. After slicing the apples dip them in lemon juice and make up the dish in the same way. Cover the dish and chill until required. Cook as above and serve hot. If wishing to serve cold, cook the dish, cool, cover and chill in the refrigerator until 30 minutes before required.

Orange salad

METRIC/IMPERIAL
6 juicy oranges
100 g/4 oz sugar
2 tablespoons rum, brandy or Cointreau
AMERICAN
6 juicy oranges
½ cup sugar
2 tablespoons rum, brandy or Cointreau

Pare the rind from 1 orange very thinly, taking care not to include any pith. Cut the rind into very fine strips. Reserve. Peel the remaining oranges and the pared orange thickly, removing all the pith and as much of the inner skin as possible. Divide the oranges into segments and cut away all the skin encasing the segments. Remove any pips (seeds).

Put the orange segments in a bowl. Put the sugar and fine strips of orange rind in a saucepan and heat gently, until the sugar has turned golden brown and begins to bubble, stirring occasionally. Pour quickly over the oranges. It will set to a hard toffee at first, then gradually dissolve in the juice of the oranges. Taste for sweetness and add the rum, brandy or liqueur. Spoon into a glass serving dish and serve with sweet biscuits (cookies) and single (light) cream.

Prepare ahead. Add the rum, brandy or liqueur, cover the dish tightly and chill in the refrigerator until 15 minutes before required. Serve as above.

Freeze. Wrap, seal, label and freeze. Thaw for 4 to 5 hours at room temperature.

Apple and chocolate crunch pudding

Orange whip

METRIC/IMPERIAL
300 ml/½ pint unsweetened yogurt
250 ml/8 fl oz orange juice
3 teaspoons powdered gelatine
grated rind of ½ orange
2 oranges, peeled, pith removed and separated into segments
2 egg whites
AMERICAN
1¼ cups unsweetened yogurt
1 cup orange juice
1 envelope unflavored gelatin
grated rind of ½ orange
2 oranges, peeled, pith removed and separated into segments
2 egg whites

Place the yogurt and 175 ml/6 fl oz/¾ cup of the orange juice in an electric blender and blend until well mixed. Sprinkle the gelatin(e) over the remaining orange juice in a small bowl and place in a pan of hot water. Heat gently until the gelatin(e) has dissolved.

Mix together the yogurt mixture, gelatin(e) mixture, orange rind and the orange segments. Leave in a cool place until just beginning to set.

Beat the egg whites until stiff and carefully fold into the orange mixture, spoon into individual glasses and leave in a cool place to set. Serve chilled.

Prepare ahead. Spoon into glasses, cover with plastic wrap and chill until 15 minutes before required.

Rhubarb fool

METRIC/IMPERIAL
700 g/1½ lb rhubarb, cut into 2.5 cm/
  1 inch pieces
100 g/4 oz sugar
150 ml/¼ pint freshly made custard
150 ml/¼ pint double cream, lightly
  beaten
Decoration:
150 ml/¼ pint fresh double cream,
  whipped
toasted chopped nuts
AMERICAN
1½ lb rhubarb, cut into 1 inch pieces
½ cup sugar
⅔ cup freshly made custard
⅔ cup heavy cream, lightly beaten
Decoration:
⅔ cup heavy cream, whipped
toasted chopped nuts

Place the rhubarb in a pan with a little water, cover and cook for 10 to 12 minutes or until tender. Add the sugar and stir well until dissolved, taste and add more sugar if necessary. Rub the fruit through a nylon sieve into a bowl or purée in an electric blender. Stir in the custard and fold in the cream. Pour into individual dishes or a glass serving dish and leave until cold. Decorate with the cream and nuts.
Prepare ahead. Pour the mixture into serving dishes, cover with plastic wrap and chill in the refrigerator until 30 minutes before required. Decorate as above.

Crème brûlée

METRIC/IMPERIAL
600 ml/1 pint fresh double cream
¼ teaspoon vanilla essence
4 egg yolks
4 tablespoons caster sugar
AMERICAN
2½ cups heavy cream
¼ teaspoon vanilla extract
4 egg yolks
4 tablespoons sugar

Heat the cream and vanilla to just below boiling point in a saucepan. Beat together the egg yolks and 1 tablespoon of the sugar until pale and creamy. Pour the hot cream onto the egg mixture, beating well. Return the mixture to the pan and cook, very gently, until the custard thickens. Do not allow to boil or try to hurry the thickening process. You

may find it easier to use a double saucepan or a bowl over a saucepan of hot water. Pour the thickened custard into a shallow heatproof dish and leave until completely cold.

Prepare a hot grill (broiler). Sprinkle the remaining sugar over the custard and place under the grill (broiler) to melt the sugar. When the sugar has melted and caramelized, remove from the heat and chill for at least 1 hour. Serve with soft fresh fruit, such as strawberries, raspberries or peaches.
Prepare ahead. When the brûlée is completely cold, cover with plastic wrap and chill in the refrigerator until required.

Cherries jubilee

METRIC/IMPERIAL
500 g/1 lb fresh black cherries, stones
  removed, or 1 × 425 g/15 oz can
  stoned black cherries, drained and juice
  reserved
300 ml/½ pint water
4 tablespoons sugar
5 cm/2 inch piece cinnamon stick
juice and grated rind of ½ orange
2 teaspoons arrowroot
4 tablespoons cherry brandy or sweet
  sherry
vanilla ice cream

Cherries jubilee

AMERICAN
1 lb fresh or canned pitted bing cherries,
  reserve the juice if using canned
1¼ cups water
4 tablespoons sugar
2 inch piece cinnamon stick
juice and grated rind of ½ orange
2 teaspoons arrowroot
4 tablespoons cherry brandy or sweet
  sherry
vanilla ice cream

If using fresh cherries, put in a pan, add the water, bring to the boil and simmer for 2 minutes or until tender but still whole. Using a slotted spoon remove the cherries. Add the sugar to the juice and stir until dissolved.

If using canned cherries, put the cherries on one side. Make up the reserved juice to 300 ml/½ pint/1¼ cups, add half the sugar or to taste, and stir until dissolved.

To either cherry juice, add the cinnamon and orange juice and rind and boil rapidly until slightly reduced.

Mix the arrowroot to a smooth paste with a little water, stir into the sauce, bring to the boil, stirring, and cook for 3 minutes. Stir in the cherry brandy or sherry and the cherries. Heat through for 1 minute.

Pour the cherries and sauce over individual portions of ice cream and serve immediately.
Note. If you prefer a cold sauce with the ice cream, stir in the cherry brandy or sherry and cherries and leave to cool before serving.

Baking

There's always a time when a few homemade treats are welcomed – when the children come home from school feeling hungry and it's not time for their meal, or when a friend pops in for a cup of tea or coffee. Biscuits (cookies) and cakes make easy-to-prepare sweets too; the children will love eating brownies with ice cream. When you're entertaining, serve crisp plain biscuits (cookies) with creamy light soufflés or mousses. Some of the biscuits (cookies) are sandwiched with a filling or have a topping, but if you're short of time omit these extra steps – plain ones will still taste good.

Before storing biscuits (cookies) and cakes cool them on a wire rack. Although homemade biscuits (cookies) or cakes will not last as long as bought ones, store them in an airtight tin to keep them fresh for as long as possible. If a tin is not quite airtight, clamp the lid down with a collar of aluminium foil. Alternatively store baked goods in a plastic box.

When you have a little extra time for cooking, home-baked bread – with its appetizing aroma, warmth and super flavour – is a real treat.

Scotch gingerbread

METRIC/IMPERIAL
100 g/4 oz butter or margarine
175 g/6 oz black treacle
50 g/2 oz golden syrup
125 g/4 oz dark brown sugar
6 tablespoons milk
2 eggs, lightly beaten
225 g/8 oz flour
¼ teaspoon salt
1 teaspoon bicarbonate of soda
1 tablespoon ground ginger
1 teaspoon cinnamon
½ teaspoon ground mixed spice

AMERICAN
½ cup butter or margarine
½ cup molasses
¼ cup golden or light corn syrup
⅔ cup dark brown sugar
6 tablespoons milk
2 eggs, lightly beaten
2 cups flour
¼ teaspoon salt
1 teaspoon baking soda
1 tablespoon ground ginger
1 teaspoon ground cinnamon
½ teaspoon mixed spice

Melt the butter or margarine, treacle (molasses), syrup and brown sugar in a small saucepan over gentle heat, stirring until well blended and the sugar has dissolved. Cool slightly, then blend in the milk and eggs.

Sift the flour, salt, soda, ginger, cinnamon and mixed spice into a mixing bowl. Pour in the contents of the saucepan and beat with a wooden spoon until the batter is smooth and well blended.

Grease a 20 cm/8 inch square cake tin (pan) and line with greased greaseproof (parchment) paper. Pour in the batter and bake in a moderate oven, 160°C/325°F, Gas Mark 3 for 1 hour or until a skewer inserted in the centre of the cake comes out clean. Allow the gingerbread to cool for 10 minutes in the tin, turn out onto a wire rack and cool completely before removing the paper. Serve cut into squares.

Prepare ahead. This gingerbread improves with keeping; wrap in clean greaseproof (waxed) paper and either put in an airtight tin or wrap completely in aluminium foil.

Makes 12–16 squares.

Wholewheat bread

METRIC/IMPERIAL
20 g/¾ oz fresh yeast
450 ml/¾ pint plus 3 tablespoons warm
water
1 kg/2 lb wholewheat flour
1 teaspoon salt
25 g/1 oz brown sugar
AMERICAN
¾ oz compressed yeast
2 cups plus 3 tablespoons warm water
8 cups wholewheat flour
1 teaspoon salt
2 tablespoons brown sugar

Mix together the yeast and the 3 tablespoons of warm water. Leave until frothy, about 5 minutes. Sift the flour and salt into a mixing bowl and stir in the sugar. Make a well in the centre and pour in the yeast mixture and the remaining warm water. Draw the ingredients together with your hands and beat until the dough comes away from the sides of the bowl, leaving it clean.

Turn the dough onto a lightly floured surface and knead for 8 to 10 minutes or until smooth and elastic. Place in a clean bowl, cover with an oiled polythene (plastic) bag and leave in a warm place for 1½ hours or until doubled in bulk.

Turn onto a lightly floured surface and knead gently for 3 minutes until smooth. Shape the dough into a loaf and place in a well-greased 1 kg/2 lb loaf tin (pan). Put into an oiled polythene (plastic) bag and leave in a warm place for about 30 minutes or until it has risen to the top of the tin. Remove the tin (pan) from the bag and bake in a hot oven 230°C/450°F, Gas Mark 8 for 20 minutes. Reduce the temperature to moderately hot, 200°C/400°F, Gas Mark 6 and cook for a further 25 to 30 minutes or until the base of the loaf sounds hollow when tapped.

Remove the loaf from the tin (pan) and cool completely on a wire rack.

Note. If preferred, shape the dough into a plait or round, sprinkle with poppy seeds and cook on a baking sheet. Alternatively, break the dough into 24 equal-sized pieces and shape into plain or fancy roll shapes. Bake rolls in a hot oven, 230°C/450°F, Gas Mark 8 for about 20 minutes or until the bases sound hollow when tapped.

Wholewheat bread

Prepare ahead. After making and kneading the dough place it in a clean bowl, cover with an oiled polythene (plastic) bag and place in the refrigerator for 8 hours or overnight. By this time the dough should have doubled in bulk and be ready for shaping.

Makes one 1 kg/2 lb loaf.

Coffee mallow creams

METRIC/IMPERIAL
75 g/3 oz butter
75 g/3 oz caster sugar
1 egg, separated
1 tablespoon instant coffee powder
2 tablespoons milk
175 g/6 oz plain flour
½ teaspoon ground cinnamon
½ teaspoon salt
1 tablespoon golden syrup
butter icing made with 100 g/4 oz butter and 175 g/6 oz icing sugar
walnut halves to decorate
AMERICAN
⅓ cup butter
⅓ cup sugar
1 egg, separated
1 tablespoon instant coffee powder
2 tablespoons milk
1½ cups flour
½ teaspoon ground cinnamon
½ teaspoon salt
1 tablespoon light corn syrup
butter icing made with ½ cup butter and 1¼ cups confectioners' sugar
walnut halves to decorate

Beat the butter and sugar together in a mixing bowl until light and fluffy. Beat in the egg yolk. Dissolve the coffee powder in the milk and stir into the creamed mixture. Sift together the flour, cinnamon and salt and stir into the creamed mixture, adding a little more milk, if necessary, to make a soft dough.

Turn the mixture onto a floured board and roll to 1 cm/½ inch thickness. Cut the dough into rounds with a 3.5 cm/1½ inch cutter. Re-roll the trimmings. Place on a baking sheet, prick with a fork and bake in a moderate oven, 180°C/350°F, Gas Mark 4 for 10 to 12 minutes or until lightly set but not firm. Cool for 5 minutes then transfer to a wire rack to cool completely.

Meanwhile, whisk the egg white and syrup together in a bowl set over a pan

of hot water until pale, fluffy and thick. Sandwich the biscuits (cookies) together with butter icing and spread the tops with the mallow mixture. Place a walnut half on top and serve.

Prepare ahead. When the biscuits (cookies) are completely cold store them in an airtight container until required. Finish and serve as above.

Makes about 12 biscuits (cookies).

Chocolate spice biscuits (cookies)

METRIC/IMPERIAL
225 g/8 oz butter
100 g/4 oz caster sugar
225 g/8 oz self-raising flour
½ teaspoon ground cinnamon
¼ teaspoon ground ginger
¼ teaspoon ground black pepper
50 g/2 oz chocolate powder
1 teaspoon vanilla essence
1 tablespoon milk
AMERICAN
1 cup butter
½ cup sugar
2 cups flour sifted with 2 teaspoons baking powder
½ teaspoon ground cinnamon
¼ teaspoon ground ginger
¼ teaspoon ground black pepper
½ cup sweetened cocoa
1 teaspoon vanilla extract
1 tablespoon milk

Beat together the butter and sugar in a mixing bowl until light and fluffy. Sift together the flour, cinnamon, ginger, pepper and chocolate powder and stir into the creamed mixture. Add the vanilla essence and milk and stir until just mixed.

Place heaped teaspoonfuls of the mixture onto greased baking sheets spacing them about 5 cm/2 inches apart and flatten slightly with a fork. Bake in a moderate oven, 180°C/350°F, Gas Mark 4 for 10 to 12 minutes or until set but not firm. Allow to cool for 5 minutes, transfer to a wire rack and cool completely. Serve on their own or sandwiched together with a little butter cream.

Prepare ahead. Cool completely and store in an airtight container. Sandwich together with butter cream, if liked, just before serving.

Makes about 12 biscuits (cookies).

Ginger cake

METRIC/IMPERIAL
225 g/8 oz self-raising flour
½ teaspoon bicarbonate of soda
½ teaspoon mixed spice or allspice
½ teaspoon ground cinnamon
1 teaspoon ground ginger
50 g/2 oz caster sugar
2 eggs
100 g/4 oz butter or margarine
175 g/6 oz golden syrup
75 g/3 oz black treacle
150 ml/¼ pint milk
AMERICAN
2 cups flour
½ teaspoon baking soda
½ teaspoon mixed spice or allspice
½ teaspoon ground cinnamon
1 teaspoon ground ginger
¼ cup sugar
2 eggs
½ cup butter or margarine
½ cup light corn syrup
¼ cup molasses
⅔ cup milk

Sift the flour, soda and spices into a mixing bowl. Stir in the sugar and the eggs. Place the butter or margarine, syrup, treacle (molasses) and milk in a saucepan and heat gently until the fat has melted and the mixture is well blended. Pour onto the egg mixture and beat vigorously to make a thick smooth batter.

Pour into a greased and lined 18 cm/7 inch square cake tin (pan) and bake in a moderate oven, 180°C/350°F, Gas Mark 4 for 1¼ hours or until a skewer inserted in the centre comes out clean. Leave in the tin for 5 minutes, turn out onto a wire tray to cool and remove the paper. Serve cut into slices or squares.

Prepare ahead. Cool completely, wrap in aluminium foil and store until required. Keeps for up to 7 days.

Makes one 18 cm/7 inch cake.

Chocolate chip cookies

METRIC/IMPERIAL
200 g/7 oz flour
½ teaspoon baking powder
¼ teaspoon salt
100 g/4 oz butter
100 g/4 oz caster sugar
2 tablespoons golden syrup
1 egg, lightly beaten
100 g/4 oz chocolate polka dots, or plain
    chocolate cut into small chips
AMERICAN
1¾ cups flour
½ teaspoon baking powder
¼ teaspoon salt
½ cup butter
½ cup sugar
2 tablespoons golden or light corn syrup
1 egg, lightly beaten
¼ lb chocolate chips or morsels

Sift the flour, baking powder and salt together. Cream the butter, sugar and syrup together until light and fluffy. Beat in the egg and stir in the flour mixture until well mixed. Stir in the chocolate pieces.

Place teaspoonfuls of the mixture on well-greased baking sheets, leaving plenty of space between each to allow for spreading during cooking. Bake in a moderately hot oven, 190°C/375°F, Gas Mark 5 for 12 to 15 minutes or until golden brown on the edges.

Cool for a few minutes. Lift the cookies carefully off the baking sheets with a palette knife and leave to cool on a wire rack.

Prepare ahead. Stack the cookies upright side by side in a roll shape and completely cover in aluminium foil or store them in an airtight tin.

Makes about 30 cookies.

Brownies

METRIC/IMPERIAL
75 g/3 oz butter
75 g/3 oz caster sugar
1 egg, lightly beaten
100 g/4 oz flour
⅛ teaspoon salt
¼ teaspoon baking powder
75 g/3 oz plain chocolate, melted in
    1 tablespoon milk
100 g/4 oz shelled walnuts, roughly
    chopped

AMERICAN
⅓ cup butter
⅓ cup sugar
1 egg, lightly beaten
1 cup flour
⅛ teaspoon salt
¼ teaspoon baking powder
3 squares semi-sweet chocolate melted in
    1 tablespoon milk
1 cup shelled walnuts, roughly chopped

Cream the butter and sugar together until light and fluffy, then beat in the egg. Sift the flour, salt and baking powder onto the creamed mixture and stir in. Stir in the melted chocolate and the walnuts until well mixed.

Grease a 20 cm/8 inch square deep cake tin (pan) and pour in the mixture. Bake in a moderate oven, 180°C/350°F, Gas Mark 4 for 25 to 30 minutes or until a skewer inserted in the centre of the cake comes out clean. Cool in the tin for 10 minutes, turn out and cut into squares while still warm and leave to cool completely.

Prepare ahead. Wrap the brownies in aluminium foil and store in an airtight container.

Makes 12–16 squares.

American cookies

METRIC/IMPERIAL
300 g/11 oz plain flour
2½ teaspoons baking powder
¼ teaspoon salt
½ teaspoon ground cumin
75 g/3 oz brown sugar
2 teaspoons grated orange rind
150 g/5 oz butter or margarine, cut into
    small pieces
2 eggs
2 tablespoons milk
AMERICAN
2¾ cups flour
2½ teaspoons baking powder
¼ teaspoon salt
½ teaspoon ground cumin
½ cup brown sugar
2 teaspoons grated orange rind
⅔ cup butter or margarine, cut into small
    pieces
2 eggs
2 tablespoons milk

Sift the flour, baking powder, salt and cumin into a mixing bowl. Stir in the sugar and rind. Add the butter or margarine and rub in until the mixture resembles fine breadcrumbs. Stir in the eggs and milk to make a firm dough.

Place spoonfuls of the mixture onto greased baking sheets, about 2.5 cm/ 1 inch apart. Bake in a moderate oven, 180°C/350°F, Gas Mark 4 for 15 minutes or until light golden brown just round the edges. Cool for 3 minutes and transfer to a wire rack to cool completely. **Prepare ahead.** Cool completely and store in an airtight container until required.

Makes about 45 cookies.

Christmas stars

METRIC/IMPERIAL
2 egg whites
175 g/6 oz caster sugar
150 g/5 oz ground almonds
1 teaspoon ground mixed spice
½ teaspoon ground ginger
finely grated rind of ½ lemon
Icing:
1 egg white
100 g/4 oz icing sugar
squeeze of lemon juice
coloured sugar strands or hundreds and
    thousands
AMERICAN
2 egg whites
¾ cup sugar
1¼ cups ground almonds
1 teaspoon ground mixed spice
½ teaspoon ground ginger
finely grated rind of ½ lemon
Icing:
1 egg white
1 cup confectioners' sugar
squeeze of lemon juice
colored sugar or sprinkles

Whisk the egg whites until stiff, then add all but 2 tablespoons of the sugar and beat until thick. Beat in the ground almonds, mixed spice, ginger and lemon rind. Chill the mixture for about 1 hour in the refrigerator.

Sprinkle about half the remaining sugar onto a working surface. Flatten the chilled dough onto the surface, then sprinkle on the remaining sugar. Roll out very thinly, then cut into stars or other shapes with fancy cutters. Place shapes on greased baking sheets and bake in a moderately hot oven, 190°C/375°F, Gas Mark 5 for 10 to 15 minutes or until they are pale brown. Cool for a few minutes. Lift the biscuits (cookies) carefully off the baking sheet with a palette knife and leave to cool on a wire rack.

Make the icing: stir the egg white and icing (confectioners') sugar together, adding a little lemon juice to make a thick icing. Spread the icing thickly on the biscuits (cookies), then sprinkle over the sugar strands (coloured sugar) or hundreds and thousands (sprinkles). Serve with tea or coffee or hang, as sweet treats, from the Christmas tree.

Prepare ahead. Store the biscuits (cookies) in an airtight container until required.

Makes about 20 biscuits (cookies).

Carolina cookies

METRIC/IMPERIAL
225 g/8 oz butter or margarine
175 g/6 oz light brown sugar
1 egg white
2 teaspoons ground cinnamon
1 teaspoon ground coriander
¼ teaspoon salt
275 g/10 oz flour, sifted

AMERICAN
1 cup butter or margarine
1 cup light brown sugar
1 egg white
2 teaspoons ground cinnamon
1 teaspoon ground coriander
¼ teaspoon salt
2½ cups flour, sifted

Cream the butter or margarine and sugar together until light and fluffy, then add the egg white, cinnamon, coriander and salt and beat until the mixture is creamy. Beat in the flour. Spread the mixture very thinly onto 3 or 4 well-greased baking sheets with a floured palette knife. Bake in a moderately hot oven, 190°C/375°F, Gas Mark 5 for about 15 minutes or until pale brown.

Cut the biscuits (cookies) into square or diamond shapes while on the baking sheets and cool for a few minutes. Transfer to a wire rack to cool completely.

Prepare ahead. Store in an airtight container.

Makes 30–40 cookies.

Butterscotch cookies

METRIC/IMPERIAL
100 g/4 oz butter, melted
175 g/6 oz soft light brown sugar
2 eggs
¼ teaspoon salt
75 g/3 oz self-raising flour
25 g/1 oz rolled oats
25 g/1 oz blanched chopped almonds

AMERICAN
½ cup butter, melted
1 cup soft light brown sugar
2 eggs
¼ teaspoon salt
¾ cup flour sifted with 1 teaspoon baking powder
⅓ cup rolled oats
3 tablespoons blanched chopped almonds

Place the butter, sugar, eggs, salt, flour and oats in a mixing bowl and beat vigorously until well mixed. Stir in the almonds. Pour the batter into a greased and lined 20 cm/8 inch square baking tin (pan) and bake in a moderate oven, 180°C/350°F, Gas Mark 4 for 20 to 25 minutes or until the top is just firm.

Cool slightly, turn out onto a wire rack, remove the paper and cool completely. Serve cut into squares.

Prepare ahead. Cool completely, wrap in aluminium foil and store until required.

Makes about 16 cookies.

Chocolate chip cookies; Christmas stars; Carolina cookies

Honey sponge

METRIC/IMPERIAL
100 g/4 oz butter or margarine, softened
100 g/4 oz caster sugar
2 teaspoons clear honey
2 eggs
½ teaspoon ground ginger
225 g/8 oz self-raising flour
½ teaspoon baking powder
75 g/3 oz shelled walnuts, finely chopped
Filling:
100 g/4 oz butter, softened
175 g/6 oz icing sugar, sifted
1 tablespoon clear honey
25 g/1 oz almonds or walnuts, chopped
grated rind of 1 lemon
2 teaspoons lemon juice
Decoration:
150 ml/¼ pint whipped cream
a few almonds or walnuts
AMERICAN
½ cup butter or margarine, softened
½ cup sugar
2 teaspoons clear honey
2 eggs
½ teaspoon ground ginger
2 cups flour sifted with 2½ teaspoons
    baking powder
½ cup shelled chopped walnuts
Filling:
½ cup butter, softened
1⅓ cups confectioners' sugar, sifted
1 tablespoon clear honey
3 tablespoons chopped almonds or walnuts
grated rind of 1 lemon
2 teaspoons lemon juice
Decoration:
⅔ cup whipped cream
a few almonds or walnuts

Beat the butter or margarine and sugar
together in a mixing bowl until light and
fluffy. Beat in the honey and the eggs one
at a time, beating well after each addition. Sift the ginger, flour and baking
powder onto the mixture and, using a
large metal spoon, fold in until well
mixed. Fold in the walnuts and spoon the
mixture into two 20 cm/8 inch lined and
greased sandwich tins (layer cake pans).
Bake in a moderate oven, 180°C/350°F,
Gas Mark 4 for 20 to 30 minutes or until
golden and springy to the touch.

Leave to cool for a few minutes then
turn out onto a wire rack to cool
completely.

Honey sponge; Banana teabread; Honey squares

Meanwhile, cream the butter and icing (confectioners') sugar together until light and fluffy. Beat in the honey, nuts, and lemon rind and juice. When the cakes are cold spread the filling over one, place the other on top and decorate the cake with the whipped cream and nuts.

Prepare ahead. Sandwich the cake together with the filling and wrap completely in aluminium foil. Store until required. Decorate as above.

Makes one 20 cm/8 inch cake.

Banana teabread

METRIC/IMPERIAL
100 g/4 oz butter or margarine, softened
100 g/4 oz caster sugar
2 eggs
1 tablespoon clear honey
225 g/8 oz self-raising flour
½ teaspoon ground cinnamon
½ teaspoon salt
50 g/2 oz shelled walnuts, chopped
75 g/3 oz sultanas
50 g/2 oz glacé cherries, halved
2 large bananas, peeled and chopped
juice of 1 lemon
1 teaspoon grated orange rind
AMERICAN
½ cup butter or margarine, softened
½ cup sugar
2 eggs
1 tablespoon clear honey
2 cups flour sifted with 2 teaspoons baking powder
½ teaspoon ground cinnamon
½ teaspoon salt
⅓ cup shelled chopped walnuts
½ cup golden raisins
⅓ cup candied cherries, halved
2 large bananas, peeled and chopped
juice of 1 lemon
1 teaspoon grated orange rind

Beat the butter or margarine and sugar together until light and fluffy. Beat in the eggs one at a time, beating well after each addition. Stir in the honey. Sift together the flour, cinnamon and salt and, with a metal spoon, fold into the creamed mixture. Stir in the walnuts, sultanas (golden raisins), cherries, banana, lemon juice and orange rind until just mixed.

Spoon the mixture into a greased 23 cm/9 inch loaf tin (pan) and bake in a moderate oven, 180°C/350°F, Gas Mark 4 for 1 hour. Reduce the temperature to 160°C/325°F, Gas Mark 3 and bake for a further 30 minutes or until a skewer

inserted in the centre comes out clean. Cool slightly and turn out onto a wire rack to cool completely. Serve sliced, and buttered, if liked.

Prepare ahead. Cool completely, cover the loaf completely in aluminium foil and store until required. Keeps well for up to 5 days.

Makes one 23 cm/9 inch loaf.

Honey squares

METRIC/IMPERIAL
200 g/7 oz self-raising flour
¼ teaspoon mixed spice or allspice
½ teaspoon salt
100 g/4 oz brown sugar
150 g/5 oz butter
175 g/6 oz clear honey
1 tablespoon water
2 eggs, beaten
Topping:
6 tablespoons clear honey
3 tablespoons blanched flaked almonds
AMERICAN
1¾ cups flour sifted with 2 teaspoons baking powder
¼ teaspoon mixed spice or allspice
½ teaspoon salt
⅔ cup brown sugar
⅔ cup butter
½ cup clear honey
1 tablespoon water
2 eggs, beaten
Topping:
6 tablespoons clear honey
3 tablespoons blanched slivered almonds

Sift the flour, spice and salt into a mixing bowl. In a saucepan mix together the sugar, butter and honey and stir over low heat until melted. Don't let the mixture come to the boil. Pour onto the flour mixture, add the water and the eggs and beat vigorously to make a smooth batter. Pour into a greased and lined 28 × 18 cm/11 × 7 inch baking tin (pan) and bake in a moderate oven, 180°C/350°F, Gas Mark 4 for 30 to 35 minutes or until golden brown and a skewer inserted in the centre comes out clean. Cool slightly, turn out onto a wire rack and leave to cool completely. Remove the paper. Place the cake on a serving plate, spread over the honey and scatter over the almonds. Cut into squares.

Prepare ahead. Cool completely, wrap in aluminium foil and store until required.

Makes about 12 squares.

Granny's fruit cake

METRIC/IMPERIAL
225 g/8 oz self-raising flour
¼ teaspoon salt
½ teaspoon ground allspice or mixed spice
½ teaspoon ground cinnamon
175 g/6 oz butter or margarine, cut into small pieces
175 g/6 oz dark brown sugar
175 g/6 oz seedless raisins
175 g/6 oz sultanas
50 g/2 oz candied peel, chopped
50 g/2 oz glacé cherries, quartered
3 eggs, beaten
2 tablespoons black treacle or golden syrup
a little milk, if necessary
AMERICAN
2 cups flour sifted with 1 tablespoon baking powder
¼ teaspoon salt
½ teaspoon ground allspice or mixed spice
½ teaspoon ground cinnamon
¾ cup butter or margarine, cut into small pieces
1 cup dark brown sugar
1 cup seedless raisins
1 cup golden raisins
⅓ cup chopped candied peel
¼ cup candied cherries, quartered
3 eggs, beaten
2 tablespoons molasses or golden or light corn syrup
a little milk, if necessary

Sift the flour, salt and spices together into a mixing bowl, then rub in the butter or margarine. Stir in the sugar, dried fruit, candied peel and cherries. Beat in the eggs a little at a time and stir in the treacle (molasses) or syrup. If the mixture seems too dry, stir in a little milk. The mixture should just drop from the spoon when shaken.

Grease a 1 kg/2 lb loaf tin (pan) and line with greased greaseproof (parchment) paper. Spoon the mixture into the tin (pan). Bake in a moderate oven, 160°C/325°F, Gas Mark 3 for 1½ hours or until a skewer inserted in the centre comes out clean. Cover the top of the cake with greaseproof (parchment) paper if it becomes too brown during cooking. Cool in the tin (pan) for 10 minutes, turn out onto a wire rack, leave until cold and remove the paper. Serve cut into slices.

Prepare ahead. Cool completely and cover with aluminium foil. Keep in an airtight container until required.

Makes one 1 kg/2 lb loaf.

Scones (baking powder biscuits)

METRIC/IMPERIAL
225 g/8 oz self-raising flour
¼ teaspoon salt
50 g/2 oz butter, cut into small pieces
50 g/2 oz caster sugar
about 150 ml/¼ pint milk
AMERICAN
2 cups flour, sifted with 1 tablespoon
baking powder
¼ teaspoon salt
¼ cup butter, cut into small pieces
¼ cup sugar
about ⅔ cup milk

Sift the flour and salt into a mixing bowl. Add the butter and rub in until the mixture resembles breadcrumbs. Stir in the sugar and enough milk to make a soft, not sticky, dough.

On a lightly floured surface, lightly knead the dough, then roll out to about 1 cm/½ inch thick and cut into circles with a 6.5 cm/2½ inch cutter. Reroll trimmings and cut out. Place on a baking sheet and cook in a hot oven, 220°C/425°F, Gas Mark 7 for 10 minutes or until risen and lightly browned around the edges. Cool on a wire rack. Best served as soon as they are cold.
Note. Add 50 g/2 oz/⅓ cup dried fruit when you stir in the sugar, if liked.

Makes about 8 scones (baking powder biscuits).

Truffles

METRIC/IMPERIAL
100 g/4 oz plain chocolate, broken into
pieces
1 tablespoon milk
1 tablespoon golden syrup
100 g/4 oz unsalted butter
100 g/4 oz icing sugar, sifted
2 teaspoons powdered instant coffee
50 g/2 oz unsweetened cocoa powder
AMERICAN
4 squares semi-sweet chocolate, broken
into pieces
1 tablespoon milk
1 tablespoon golden or light corn syrup
½ cup unsalted butter
⅔ cup confectioners' sugar, sifted
2 teaspoons powdered instant coffee
½ cup unsweetened cocoa

Put the chocolate, milk and syrup in a small pan, heat gently until melted, do not allow to boil, then cool slightly. Beat the butter, icing (confectioners') sugar, coffee powder and half the cocoa powder together until light and fluffy, then slowly beat in the melted chocolate mixture and continue beating until the mixture is pale and smooth.

Leave the mixture to set in the refrigerator for 1 hour, then roll lightly into walnut-sized balls. Roll the balls in the remaining cocoa powder. Place in small sweet papers and store in a box in a cool place until required. These make ideal homemade gifts.

Makes 12–16 truffles.

Scones (baking powder biscuits)

72

Entertaining

For dinner parties and other special occasions, the dishes you serve must look impressive but be simple to prepare. A tall order? No, not if you choose the menu wisely. It is essential to prepare ahead and so avoid last minute panics because you will want to be with your guests before the meal. Put the hot dishes in the oven, or on the hob, before they arrive and remember – there is nothing more inducive to a good appetite than delicious aromas wafting from the kitchen.

Always select starters to contrast with the food that follows. For the busy cook, soups are an excellent choice – they can be prepared in advance and either reheated or served cold. They are always popular and you will find a wide selection to choose from in this chapter. Cold savouries can be prepared the night before and forgotten until they need to be served. Dips accompanied by crisp vegetables make a simple, informal start to the meal.

The main dishes in this chapter look and taste special. You will find more simple ones which look after themselves in the main meals chapter. If you decide to serve simple grilled (broiled) meats or roasts, a more elaborate vegetable dish turns them into something special. Vegetable dishes are best served freshly cooked, unless otherwise stated in the recipes.

If you haven't time to bake a loaf of bread, buy a French loaf and heat it in the oven before serving, with some easily prepared herb or savoury butter.

A cold sweet will pose no problems; prepare in advance and chill until half-an-hour or so before required. If you feel you have enough last minute things to do, don't choose a sweet that requires decorating just before serving. If you choose a pie, pop it in the oven as you sit down to your main course; you may have to wait a few minutes for it to brown but you'll find your guests will be glad of a breathing space.

Aubergine (eggplant) dip

METRIC/IMPERIAL
2 aubergines
1 garlic clove, crushed
4 tablespoons olive oil
juice of 1 lemon
salt and pepper
1 tablespoon chopped fresh parsley
½ teaspoon fennel seeds, crushed

AMERICAN
2 eggplant
1 garlic clove, minced
4 tablespoons olive oil
juice of 1 lemon
salt and pepper
1 tablespoon chopped fresh parsley
½ teaspoon fennel seeds, minced

Cook the aubergines (eggplant) in boiling salted water for 15 minutes or until tender. Drain, peel the aubergines (eggplant) and chop the flesh roughly. Place the flesh, garlic, oil and juice in an electric blender and blend until smooth. Add salt and pepper to taste, the parsley and fennel seeds and blend to mix. Transfer the mixture to a serving dish, cover and chill until 15 minutes before required. Serve with raw green or red peppers, spring onions (scallions), cubes of cheese and blanched green beans.

Avocado dip

METRIC/IMPERIAL
2 avocados
3 tablespoons mayonnaise
salt and pepper
pinch of cayenne pepper
1 small onion, very finely chopped
2 teaspoons oil
2 teaspoons wine vinegar
AMERICAN
2 avocados
3 tablespoons mayonnaise
salt and pepper
pinch of cayenne pepper
1 small onion, very finely chopped
2 teaspoons oil
2 teaspoons wine vinegar

Peel the avocados, remove the stones
(pits) and chop roughly. Beat together
the avocados, mayonnaise, salt and pepper to taste, cayenne, onion, oil and
vinegar until well mixed. Alternatively,
place the ingredients in an electric blender and blend until smooth. Spoon the
mixture into a serving dish, cover and
chill for 15 minutes (if you keep it longer
the dip will start to turn brown). Serve
with peeled prawns (shrimp), small raw
mushrooms and cauliflower florets.

Cream cheese dip

METRIC/IMPERIAL
175 g/6 oz cream cheese, softened
4 tablespoons fresh double cream
2 teaspoons grated horseradish
juice and grated rind of $\frac{1}{2}$ lemon
1 garlic clove, crushed
1 teaspoon chopped fresh fennel (optional)
sliced stuffed olives to garnish
AMERICAN
$\frac{3}{4}$ cup cream cheese, softened
4 tablespoons heavy cream
2 teaspoons grated horseradish
juice and grated rind of $\frac{1}{2}$ lemon
1 garlic clove, minced
1 teaspoon chopped fresh fennel (optional)
sliced stuffed olives to garnish

Beat together the cheese, cream, horseradish, lemon juice and rind, garlic and
fennel (if using) until the mixture is
smooth. Spoon into a serving dish, cover
and chill until 15 minutes before required. Garnish with olive slices. Serve
with carrot, celery and fennel sticks.

Cream cheese dip

Mayonnaise verte

METRIC/IMPERIAL
50 g/2 oz sorrel
25 g/1 oz spinach
25 g/1 oz parsley, chervil or chives
300 ml/½ pint mayonnaise
AMERICAN
2 oz sorrel
1 oz spinach
1 oz parsley, chervil or chives
1¼ cups mayonnaise

Cook the sorrel, spinach and parsley, chervil or chives in boiling water for 1 minute. Strain, squeezing out as much moisture as possible. Chop very finely or purée in an electric blender and stir into the mayonnaise. Cover and chill until required. Serve with shellfish or crisp raw vegetable sticks.

Note. For a more pungent sauce to go with vegetables, stir 2 crushed (minced) garlic cloves into the mayonnaise and accompany with herb-buttered bread.

Herb butters

METRIC/IMPERIAL
100 g/4 oz butter, softened
4 teaspoons chopped fresh herbs or 1 teaspoon dried herbs
1 teaspoon juice
AMERICAN
½ cup butter, softened
4 teaspoons chopped fresh herbs or 1 teaspoon dried herbs
1 teaspoon lemon juice

Cream the butter in a small bowl, stir in the herbs and gradually work in the lemon juice. Spoon onto a piece of aluminium foil and shape into a roll about 2.5 cm/1 inch in diameter. Roll up in the foil and chill in refrigerator until required. Cut the butter into slices and serve with bread or grilled (broiled) meats.

Note. Other flavours may be added to the butter: try pounded anchovies, tomato purée (paste), crushed (minced) garlic, onion juice, etc.

Herb butter; Mayonnaise verte

Gazpacho

METRIC/IMPERIAL
500 g/1 lb tomatoes, peeled, quartered
    and seeded
1 medium onion, chopped
½ green pepper, cored, seeded and chopped
½ red pepper, cored, seeded and chopped
½ cucumber, peeled and chopped
1 garlic clove, crushed
6 tablespoons vegetable oil
3 tablespoons lemon juice
150 ml/¼ pint chicken stock
250 ml/8 fl oz tomato juice
salt and pepper
sprigs of parsley or chervil to garnish
AMERICAN
1 lb tomatoes, peeled, quartered and seeded
1 medium onion, chopped
½ green pepper, cored, seeded and chopped
½ red pepper, cored, seeded and chopped
½ cucumber, peeled and chopped
1 garlic clove, minced
6 tablespoons vegetable oil
3 tablespoons lemon juice
⅔ cup chicken stock
1 cup tomato juice
salt and pepper
sprigs of parsley or chervil to garnish

Place half of the ingredients, with salt
and pepper to taste, in an electric blender
and blend until the mixture is smooth.
Pour into a container. Repeat the blending with the remaining ingredients and
add to the container. Cover and chill the
soup in the refrigerator until required.
Stir the soup well and pour into individual bowls or one large glass bowl.
Garnish with the parsley or chervil and
chill until required.

Gazpacho is often served with side
dishes of croûtons, chopped cucumber,
olives, peppers and onion.
Freeze. Pour into container, cover, seal,
label and freeze. Thaw overnight in the
refrigerator. Stir well before serving.

Gazpacho

Chilled cucumber soup

METRIC/IMPERIAL
225 g/8 oz Gouda or Gruyère cheese, cubed
2 cucumbers, roughly chopped
2 tablespoons lemon juice
1 tablespoon chopped fresh marjoram, fennel, chives and parsley
½ teaspoon salt
¼ teaspoon pepper
300 ml/½ pint chicken stock
AMERICAN
1⅓ cups diced Gouda or Gruyère cheese
2 cucumbers, roughly chopped
2 tablespoons lemon juice
1 tablespoon chopped fresh marjoram, fennel, chives and parsley
½ teaspoon salt
¼ teaspoon pepper
1¼ cups chicken stock

Place half of all the ingredients in an electric blender and process until thoroughly blended. Pour into a large bowl or container. Repeat the blending with the remaining ingredients and pour the mixture into the bowl or container.

Cover the bowl or container and chill in the refrigerator until 30 minutes before required. Pour into a serving dish or individual bowls.

French onion soup

METRIC/IMPERIAL
15 g/½ oz butter
1 tablespoon vegetable oil
700 g/1½ lb onions, thinly sliced into rings
40 g/1½ oz flour
1 litre/1¾ pints well-flavoured beef stock
salt and pepper
1 garlic clove, crushed
4 rounds French bread
50 g/2 oz Cheddar cheese, grated
AMERICAN
1 tablespoon butter
1 tablespoon vegetable oil
1½ lb onions, thinly sliced into rings
⅓ cup flour
4¼ cups well-flavored beef stock
salt and pepper
1 garlic clove, minced
4 rounds French bread
½ cup grated Cheddar cheese

Heat the butter and oil in a saucepan. Add the onions, cover and fry gently for 15 to 20 minutes, stirring occasionally, until soft and golden. Stir in the flour and cook for 1 minute, stirring constantly.

Gradually add the stock, stirring all the time, and bring to the boil. Season to taste. Cover the pan and simmer for 20 minutes. Add the garlic, taste and adjust the seasoning if necessary. Keep hot.

Toast the French bread on both sides. Top each round with some of the cheese and place under a hot grill (broiler) for 2 minutes or until the cheese melts and bubbles. Pour the soup into a warmed tureen and float the bread on top. Serve immediately.

Prepare ahead. Cool the soup. Pour into a container, cover and chill in the refrigerator. Reheat slowly until hot, add the garlic and continue as above.

Freeze. Don't add the garlic. Pour into a rigid container, cover, label and freeze. Thaw in a saucepan with 2 tablespoons water over very low heat. Add the garlic and continue as above.

Cream of celery soup

METRIC/IMPERIAL
50 g/2 oz butter
1 head of celery, roughly chopped
1 medium onion, chopped
900 ml/1½ pints chicken stock
¼ teaspoon grated nutmeg
1 sprig of fresh thyme
salt and pepper
25 g/1 oz cornflour
300 ml/½ pint milk
6 tablespoons fresh single cream
a little finely chopped celery to garnish
AMERICAN
¼ cup butter
1 bunch of celery, roughly chopped
1 medium onion, chopped
3¾ cups chicken stock
¼ teaspoon grated nutmeg
1 sprig of fresh thyme
salt and pepper
¼ cup cornstarch
1¼ cups milk
6 tablespoons light cream
a little finely chopped celery to garnish

Melt the butter in a large saucepan. Add the celery and onion and cook for 5 minutes or until the onion is soft. Add the stock, nutmeg, thyme and seasoning, bring to the boil, cover and simmer for 45 minutes or until the celery is very soft.

Remove the thyme and allow the soup to cool slightly. Pour half the mixture into an electric blender and purée until smooth; pour into a clean pan. Purée the remaining mixture and pour into the pan.

Mix the cornflour (cornstarch) to a smooth paste with a little of the milk and stir into the celery mixture with the remaining milk. Bring the soup to the boil, stirring constantly, and simmer for 3 minutes. Taste and adjust the seasoning if necessary.

Pour the soup into warmed bowls, stir a little of the cream into each bowl, sprinkle with a little chopped celery and serve immediately.

Prepare ahead. After simmering the soup for 3 minutes, pour into a suitable container, cover, cool and chill in the refrigerator. Reheat the soup over low heat. Taste and adjust the seasoning if necessary. Serve as above.

Freeze. Pour the purée into a container, cover, seal, label and freeze. Thaw the soup in a saucepan with some of the milk for 1 hour, stirring occasionally, until hot. Mix in cornflour (cornstarch) mixture and finish as above.

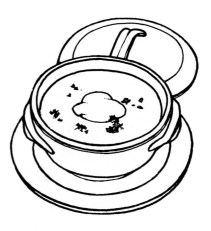

Watercress soup

METRIC/IMPERIAL
15 g/½ oz butter
2 medium onions, finely chopped
2 medium potatoes, diced
2 bunches watercress, trimmed
600 ml/1 pint chicken stock
salt and pepper
300 ml/½ pint milk
sprigs of watercress to garnish
AMERICAN
1 tablespoon butter
2 medium onions, finely chopped
2 medium potatoes, diced
4 oz watercress, trimmed
2½ cups chicken stock
salt and pepper
1¼ cups milk
sprigs of watercress to garnish

Melt the butter in a large saucepan. Add the onions and potatoes and cook for 5 minutes or until the onions are soft. Add half the watercress and cook for a further 5 minutes. Stir in the stock, season and simmer for 25 minutes or until the vegetables are very tender.

Cool slightly. Purée the mixture in an electric blender. Leave some of the purée in the blender, add the remaining watercress and chop finely. Mix in the milk and chill the soup until required, if serving cold. Pour into individual serving dishes and garnish with watercress sprigs. To serve hot, reheat over low heat until very hot and pour into a warmed serving dish. Garnish with watercress sprigs.

Prepare ahead. Pour into a container, cover, cool and chill until 30 minutes before required. Pour into dishes and serve as above.

Freeze. Don't add the milk. Pour into a rigid container, cover, label and freeze. To serve cold, thaw overnight in the refrigerator or for 4 to 5 hours at room temperature. Stir in the milk and serve. To serve hot, reheat with the milk over very low heat.

Ham and pea soup

METRIC/IMPERIAL
500 g/1 lb whole or split dried green
    peas, soaked overnight
1 large knuckle of bacon soaked overnight
    in cold water
1 medium onion, finely chopped
3 celery stalks, finely chopped
1 medium potato, diced
2·75 litres/5 pints water
3 sprigs fresh thyme
pepper
fried croûtons to garnish

AMERICAN
1 lb whole or split dried green peas, soaked
    overnight
1 large smoked ham hock, soaked
    overnight in cold water
1 medium onion, finely chopped
3 celery stalks, finely chopped
1 medium potato, diced
6 pints water
3 sprigs fresh thyme
pepper
fried croûtons to garnish

Drain the peas and put them in a large
saucepan with the drained knuckle
(hock). Add the onion, celery, potato,
water and thyme. Bring to the boil, cover
and simmer for 3 hours or until the peas
and meat are very tender. Remove and
discard the thyme. Remove the meat
from the pan. Discard any fat and bone,
dice the meat and return to the pea
mixture. Add pepper to taste. Reheat the
soup over gentle heat and when very hot
pour into a warmed tureen. Serve with
the croûtons.
Prepare ahead. Add meat to pea mixture,
cool, pour into a container, cover and
chill in the refrigerator. Reheat, season
and serve as above.
Freeze. Cool, pour into a rigid container,
cover, label and freeze. Add a little water
to a saucepan and thaw the soup over
very low heat.

Ham and pea soup; Scallop and artichoke soup

Scallop and artichoke soup

METRIC/IMPERIAL
15 g/½ oz butter
1 onion, finely chopped
700 g/1½ lb Jerusalem artichokes,
    chopped
600 ml/1 pint chicken stock
salt and pepper
225 g/8 oz scallops
150 ml/¼ pint water and dry white wine
    mixed
150 ml/¼ pint milk
¼ teaspoon grated nutmeg
1 tablespoon chopped fresh parsley to
    garnish

AMERICAN
1 tablespoon butter
1 onion, finely chopped
1½ lb Jerusalem artichokes, chopped
2½ cups chicken stock
salt and pepper
8 sea scallops
⅔ cup water and dry white wine mixed
⅔ cup milk
¼ teaspoon grated nutmeg
1 tablespoon chopped fresh parsley to
    garnish

Melt the butter in a large saucepan. Add
the onion and artichokes, cover and
cook gently for 5 minutes or until the
onion is soft. Add the stock and seasoning to taste and simmer gently for 25
minutes or until the artichokes are soft.
  Cool the mixture slightly and pour
into an electric blender. Purée until the
mixture is smooth.
  In a saucepan poach the scallops in
the water and wine mixture for 2 to 4
minutes or until just tender. Slice scallops and add, with their cooking liquid,
to the artichoke mixture. Taste and
adjust seasoning if necessary. Heat in a
saucepan, add the milk and nutmeg and
bring to just below boiling point; if the
scallops are boiled they will be tough.
  Pour the soup into a warmed tureen
and garnish with the parsley.
Prepare ahead. Combine the artichoke
and scallop mixtures, pour into a container, cover, cool and chill in the refrigerator. Reheat the soup very gently,
taste and adjust seasoning if necessary,
add the milk and nutmeg and continue
as above.
Freeze. Cool, pour into container, label
and freeze. Thaw overnight in refrigerator or for 3 to 4 hours at room
temperature. Reheat as above.

Tomato and mint soup

METRIC/IMPERIAL
25 g/1 oz butter
1 medium carrot, diced
1 medium onion, chopped
3 celery stalks, chopped
50 g/2 oz bacon, chopped
700 g/1½ lb tomatoes, peeled and chopped
450 ml/¾ pint chicken stock
300 ml/½ pint tomato juice
salt and pepper
1 teaspoon sugar
2 tablespoons chopped fresh mint
15 g/½ oz cornflour
150 ml/¼ pint milk
AMERICAN
2 tablespoons butter
1 medium carrot, diced
1 medium onion, chopped
3 celery stalks, chopped
¼ cup chopped bacon
1½ lb tomatoes, peeled and chopped
2 cups chicken stock
1¼ cups tomato juice
salt and pepper
1 teaspoon sugar
2 tablespoons chopped fresh mint
2 tablespoons cornstarch
⅔ cup milk

Melt the butter in a large saucepan. Add the carrot, onion, celery and bacon and cook for 5 minutes or until the onion is soft. Add the tomatoes and cook, stirring, for 2 minutes. Stir in the stock, tomato juice, seasoning to taste, sugar and mint. Bring to the boil, cover and simmer for 45 minutes or until the vegetables are very soft.

Cool slightly and purée the mixture in an electric blender. For a really smooth soup rub the purée through a nylon sieve. Heat the soup slowly. Mix the cornflour (cornstarch) to a smooth paste with a little of the milk and add to the soup with the remaining milk. Bring the soup to the boil, stirring constantly, and simmer for 3 minutes. Taste and adjust the seasoning if necessary.

Pour the soup into warmed bowls. Sprinkle with a little chopped fresh mint, if liked.
Note. This soup may be served chilled with a spoonful of sour(ed) cream stirred into each portion.

Prepare ahead. After simmering for 3 minutes, cool, pour into a container, cover and chill in the refrigerator until required. Reheat over low heat, if necessary.
Freeze. Purée the soup, pour into a container, cover, seal, label and freeze. Reheat in a saucepan, adding a little water if necessary, for 1 hour or until hot. Add the cornflour (cornstarch) and milk to the soup and continue as above.

Mushrooms à la Grecque

METRIC/IMPERIAL
300 ml/½ pint water
1 small onion, chopped
2 tablespoons olive oil
1 teaspoon tomato purée
salt and pepper
1 sprig thyme
½ teaspoon dried marjoram
juice of ½ lemon
350 g/12 oz mushrooms, halved, or quartered if large
1 tablespoon chopped fresh parsley to garnish
AMERICAN
1¼ cups water
1 small onion, chopped
2 tablespoons olive oil
1 teaspoon tomato paste
salt and pepper
1 sprig thyme
½ teaspoon dried marjoram
juice of ½ lemon
3 cups mushrooms, halved, or quartered if large
1 tablespoon chopped fresh parsley to garnish

Put the water, onion, oil, purée (paste), seasoning to taste, herbs and lemon juice in a large saucepan and simmer for 5 minutes. Add the mushrooms and simmer gently for 10 minutes. Transfer the mushrooms with a slotted spoon to a serving dish. Boil the cooking liquid rapidly until it is reduced to about 4 tablespoons.

Discard the sprig of thyme. Pour the liquid over the mushrooms and chill in the refrigerator for 30 minutes or until required.

Serve sprinkled with the chopped parsley as a first course or as an accompaniment to plain grilled (broiled) lamb.

German vegetable soup

METRIC/IMPERIAL
40 g/1½ oz butter
1 small onion, chopped
4 large carrots, thinly sliced
½ turnip or swede, diced
2 celery stalks, sliced
2 medium potatoes, diced
1 medium leek, sliced
1·2 litres/2 pints beef stock
salt and pepper
100 g/4 oz peas
100 g/4 oz sweetcorn kernels
½ small cabbage, thinly sliced
100 g/4 oz cooked beetroot, diced
100 g/4 oz frankfurters
AMERICAN
3 tablespoons butter
1 small onion, chopped
4 large carrots, thinly sliced
½ turnip or swede, diced
2 celery stalks, sliced
2 medium potatoes, diced
1 medium leek, sliced
5 cups beef stock
salt and pepper
¾ cup peas
¾ cup kernel corn
½ small cabbage, shredded
⅔ cup diced cooked beets
¼ lb frankfurters

Melt the butter in a large saucepan. Add the onion, carrots, turnip or swede, celery, potatoes, leek, stock and seasoning to taste and simmer for 20 minutes or until the vegetables are almost tender. Add the peas, corn kernels and cabbage and simmer for a further 10 minutes. Add the beetroot (beets) and frankfurters and simmer very gently for 5 minutes or until heated through.

Pour into a warmed casserole and serve immediately with bread and cheese to make a simple supper dish.
Prepare ahead. After adding the peas, sweet corn and cabbage and simmering for 10 minutes, cool, pour into a container, cover and chill in the refrigerator. Reheat slowly until very hot, add the beetroot and frankfurters and simmer until heated through. Serve as above.

Tomato and mint soup; Mushrooms à la Grecque

Illustrated overleaf: German vegetable soup

Grilled grapefruit medley

METRIC/IMPERIAL
2 grapefruit
50 g/2 oz brown sugar
4 tablespoons brandy or medium sherry
15 g/½ oz butter
50 g/2 oz sultanas
25 g/1 oz glacé cherries, halved
¼ teaspoon ground ginger
AMERICAN
2 grapefruit
⅓ cup brown sugar
4 tablespoons brandy or medium sherry
1 tablespoon butter
⅓ cup golden raisins
⅛ cup candied cherries
¼ teaspoon ground ginger

Cut the grapefruit in halves, remove cores and loosen segments. Sprinkle with half the sugar. Sprinkle the brandy or sherry over the grapefruit halves and place under a hot grill (broiler) for 3 minutes or until hot, or if using the brandy until it flares. Meanwhile, heat the remaining sugar, the butter, sultanas (raisins), cherries and ginger and stir until well mixed and just bubbling.

Place the grapefruit halves in individual dishes and pile the fruit sauce on top. Serve immediately as a festive and warming first course.
tanas (raisins), cherries and ginger and

Left: German vegetable soup (page 81); Grilled grapefruit medley

Below: Corn-on-the-cob

Devilled eggs

METRIC/IMPERIAL
4 eggs, hard-boiled
4 stalks celery
175 g/6 oz cream cheese, softened
1 teaspoon tomato purée
salt and pepper
Sauce:
3 tablespoons Worcestershire sauce
3 tablespoons tomato ketchup
juice and grated rind of 1 lemon
few drops Tabasco sauce
1 tomato, peeled, seeded and quartered
1 teaspoon sugar
1 teaspoon vinegar
1 teaspoon prepared mustard
AMERICAN
4 hard-cooked eggs
4 stalks celery
¾ cup cream cheese, softened
1 teaspoon tomato paste
salt and pepper
Sauce:
3 tablespoons Worcestershire sauce
3 tablespoons tomato ketchup
juice and grated rind of 1 lemon
few drops Tabasco sauce
1 tomato, peeled, seeded and quartered
1 teaspoon sugar
1 teaspoon vinegar
1 teaspoon prepared mustard

Cut the eggs in half lengthways and carefully remove the yolks. Cut the celery into 7.5 cm/3 inch pieces. Arrange the egg whites and celery on a serving dish.

Put the yolks, cream cheese, tomato purée (paste) and salt and pepper to taste in an electric blender and purée until smooth; alternatively rub the ingredients through a nylon sieve. Spoon into a piping bag fitted with a fluted nozzle and pipe into the egg whites and celery.

Place all the sauce ingredients, and salt and pepper to taste, in an electric blender and blend until well mixed. Pour the sauce over the stuffed eggs and celery; serve some separately if liked.
Prepare ahead. Place the stuffed eggs and celery in a container, cover and chill for a few hours in the refrigerator. Arrange on a serving dish, make the sauce and serve as above.

Corn-on-the-cob

METRIC/IMPERIAL
4 corn cobs
salt and pepper
50 g/2 oz butter
AMERICAN
4 corn cobs
salt and pepper
¼ cup butter

Cook the corn cobs in a large pan of boiling water for 10 minutes or until tender. Lift out the cobs with a draining spoon and place on hot plates. Season generously with salt and pepper and rub the butter over the cobs until some of it melts. Serve very hot with more melted butter handed separately, if liked. Serve as a starter or with grilled (broiled) bacon and bread as a quick, filling snack.

Avocado with crab

METRIC/IMPERIAL
3 tomatoes, peeled and chopped
15 g/½ oz butter
15 g/½ oz flour
150 ml/¼ pint milk
salt and pepper
2 teaspoons tomato purée
pinch of cayenne pepper
75 g/3 oz crab meat
2 avocados
1 tablespoon lemon juice
AMERICAN
3 tomatoes, peeled and chopped
1 tablespoon butter
2 tablespoons flour
⅔ cup milk
salt and pepper
2 teaspoons tomato paste
pinch of cayenne pepper
⅓ cup crab meat
2 avocados
1 tablespoon lemon juice

Cook the tomatoes in the butter for 1 minute, add the flour and cook for 1 minute. Gradually stir in the milk to make a smooth sauce, bring to the boil, stirring, and cook for 1 minute. Stir in salt and pepper to taste, tomato purée (paste), cayenne and crab meat and mix well. Leave the sauce until completely cold.

Halve the avocados and remove the stones (pits). Rub the cut surfaces of the avocados with the lemon juice and stir any remaining juice into the sauce. Spoon the sauce into the avocado halves and serve with thin brown bread and butter as an attractive starter.

Prepare ahead. Make the sauce, cover, cool and chill until required. Cut the avocados just before serving, rub with the lemon juice and stir the remaining juice into the sauce. Serve as above.

Avocado with crab

Avocado and chicken mould

METRIC/IMPERIAL
15 g/½ oz powdered gelatine
3 tablespoons water
300 ml/½ pint apple juice
salt and pepper
2 ripe avocados
1 tablespoon lemon juice
100 g/4 oz cooked chicken, chopped, or
   chicken pâté
4 tablespoons mayonnaise
Garnish:
100 g/4 oz cream cheese, softened
lemon slices
lettuce leaves

AMERICAN
2 envelopes unflavored gelatin
3 tablespoons water
1¼ cups apple juice
salt and pepper
2 ripe avocados
1 tablespoon lemon juice
½ cup cooked chopped chicken, or chicken
   pâté
4 tablespoons mayonnaise
Garnish:
½ cup cream cheese, softened
lemon slices
lettuce leaves

Sprinkle the gelatin(e) over the water in a bowl and leave for 5 minutes. Place the bowl in a pan of hot water and heat gently until the gelatin(e) has dissolved. Stir into the apple juice and season generously. Peel the avocados, place the flesh, lemon juice, chicken and mayonnaise in an electric blender and blend until smooth. Slowly pour in the gelatin(e) mixture and blend thoroughly. Alternatively, beat together the avocado flesh, lemon juice and mayonnaise until smooth. Beat in the pâté, if using, or beat in the chicken, chopped very finely. Stir in the gelatin(e) mixture until well blended.

Pour the mixture into a lightly oiled 900 ml/1½ pint/3¾ cup mould and leave in a cool place until set.

Turn the mould onto a serving dish and decorate with piped cream cheese, lemon slices and lettuce leaves.

Prepare ahead. When the mixture is set, cover the mould completely and chill in the refrigerator until 30 minutes before required. Turn out and garnish as above.

Avocado and chicken mould

Baked smokies

METRIC/IMPERIAL
2 Arbroath smokies, or 700 g/1½ lb
    smoked haddock or mackerel
2 medium onions, finely chopped
pepper
225 g/8 oz tomatoes, sliced
300 ml/½ pint fresh double cream
25 g/1 oz hard cheese grated
AMERICAN
2 Arbroath smokies, or 1½ lb smoked
    haddock or mackerel or whitefish
2 medium onions, finely chopped
pepper
½ lb tomatoes, sliced
1¼ cups heavy cream
¼ cup grated hard cheese

Flake the flesh of the fish and put half in a casserole. Sprinkle with half the chopped onion. Add pepper to taste and repeat with the remaining fish and onion. Cover with the sliced tomatoes, pour the cream into the casserole and sprinkle the tomatoes with the cheese.

Bake in a moderate oven, 180°C/350°F, Gas Mark 4 for 30 minutes or until the top is lightly browned and the fish is cooked. Serve immediately.
Prepare ahead. Make layers with the fish and onions and pour in the cream. Cover the dish with aluminium foil and bake for 25 minutes. Cool, cover with plastic wrap or more foil and chill in the refrigerator. Remove the covering, cover the fish mixture with the tomatoes and sprinkle over the cheese. Reheat in a moderate oven, 180°C/350°F, Gas Mark 4 for 20 to 25 minutes or until the mixture is hot. If the top is not brown enough, place the dish under a hot grill (broiler) to brown.
Freeze. Assemble, wrap, seal, label and freeze. Thaw in a hot oven, 220°C/425°F, Gas Mark 7 and bake for 20 minutes. Reduce to moderate, 180°C/350°F, Gas Mark 4 and bake for a further 30 minutes or until hot.

Smoked haddock mousse; Baked smokies

Smoked haddock mousse

METRIC/IMPERIAL
500 g/1 lb smoked haddock
600 ml/1 pint milk
1 small onion, quartered
50 g/2 oz butter
50 g/2 oz flour
pinch of ground mace
15 g/½ oz gelatine
75 ml/2½ fl oz water
5 tablespoons mayonnaise
5 tablespoons fresh double cream, lightly
    whipped
salt and pepper
Garnish:
1 hard-boiled egg, sliced
few sprigs of parsley
300 ml/½ pint aspic jelly (optional)
AMERICAN
1 lb smoked haddock
2½ cups milk
1 small onion, quartered
¼ cup butter
½ cup flour
pinch of ground mace
1 envelope unflavored gelatin
⅓ cup water
⅔ cup mayonnaise
⅓ cup heavy cream, lightly whipped
salt and pepper
Garnish:
1 hard-cooked egg, sliced
few sprigs of parsley
1¼ cups aspic jelly (optional)

Place the haddock in a large saucepan and add the milk and onion. Bring the liquid to the boil, cover the pan and remove from the heat. Leave for 30 minutes. Lift out the fish and flake the flesh, removing all the skin and bones. Strain the cooking liquid and reserve.

Melt the butter in a saucepan, add the flour and cook for 1 minute, stirring constantly. Gradually stir in the reserved cooking liquid and, still stirring, bring to the boil. Stir in the mace and the flaked fish and set aside to cool.

Sprinkle the gelatin(e) over the water in a small bowl and leave for 5 minutes. Heat gently in a saucepan of hot water until the gelatin(e) has dissolved. Stir into the haddock mixture. Fold in the mayonnaise and the cream and season to taste.

Grease a 1 litre/2 pint/5 cup dish. Spoon in the mixture and leave in a cool place to set.

Decorate the top of the mousse with the egg slices and parsley. If using the aspic jelly, pour over enough to cover and leave in a cool place to set.
Prepare ahead. Cover the dish closely with aluminium foil or plastic wrap and chill in the refrigerator until required.
Freeze. Don't glaze with aspic. Wrap, seal, label and freeze. Thaw in the refrigerator overnight or for 4 to 5 hours at room temperature.

Kipper pâté

METRIC/IMPERIAL
15 g/½ oz butter
225 g/8 oz kipper fillets
225 g/8 oz cream cheese, softened
1 garlic clove, crushed
1 tablespoon grated or creamed
    horseradish
1 teaspoon finely chopped fresh fennel
juice of ½ lemon
pepper
lemon twist to garnish
AMERICAN
1 tablespoon butter
½ lb kipper fillets
1 cup cream cheese, softened
1 garlic clove, minced
1 tablespoon grated or creamed
    horseradish
1 teaspoon finely chopped fresh fennel
juice of ½ lemon
pepper
lemon twist to garnish

Melt the butter in a frying pan (skillet). Add the kipper fillets and fry gently for 10 minutes or until the flesh flakes easily. Remove the fish from the pan. Discard any skin and large bones. Place the flesh in a bowl and mash with a fork. Stir in the cheese, garlic, horseradish, fennel and lemon juice. Beat the mixture vigorously until the pâté is quite smooth. Add pepper to taste and beat again. Spoon into a serving dish, level the surface and garnish with the lemon twist. Chill before serving.
Prepare ahead. Don't add the lemon twist. Cover the dish closely with aluminium foil or plastic wrap and chill in the refrigerator until 15 minutes before required. Garnish with the lemon.
Freeze. Wrap, seal, label and freeze. Thaw overnight in the refrigerator or for 5 hours at room temperature.

Calamares salad; Taramasalata

Taramasalata

METRIC/IMPERIAL
225 g/8 oz smoked cod's roe, fresh or
    from a jar or can
2 slices white bread
1 garlic clove, peeled
juice of ½ lemon
150 ml/¼ pint olive oil
2 tablespoons cold water
pepper
AMERICAN
½ lb fresh smoked cod's roe, or 1 × ½ lb
    jar tarama
2 slices white bread
1 garlic clove, peeled
juice of ½ lemon
⅔ cup olive oil
2 tablespoons cold water
pepper

Skin the cod's roe if necessary. Soak the
bread briefly in a little cold water and
squeeze well. Put the cod's roe, bread,
garlic and lemon juice in an electric
blender and purée until smooth. Run the
blender on slow speed and gradually add
the olive oil, making sure each addition
is absorbed before adding the next. Gradually blend in the water in the same
way. Season to taste with pepper.
    Spoon into a dish and serve with hot
toast or Pita bread.
Prepare ahead. Cover and chill in the
refrigerator until 15 minutes before
required.
Freeze. Wrap, seal, label and freeze.
Thaw overnight in the refrigerator or for
4 to 5 hours at room temperature.

Chicken liver pâté

METRIC/IMPERIAL
225 g/8 oz chicken livers
100 g/4 oz butter
1 tablespoon port, sherry or Madeira
1 garlic clove, peeled
salt and pepper
1 bay leaf
AMERICAN
½ lb chicken livers
½ cup butter
1 tablespoon port, sherry or Madeira
1 garlic clove, peeled
salt and pepper
1 bay leaf

Clean the chicken livers and cut away
any greenish parts or veins. Melt half of
the butter in a frying pan (skillet). Add
the livers and cook them gently for 5
minutes, turning once, or until cooked
through but still slightly pink in the
centre.
    Transfer the livers to an electric blen-
der. Scrape any sediment from the pan
into the blender. Add the port, sherry or
Madeira and the garlic clove and blend
until the mixture is smooth. Transfer the
mixture to a bowl and beat in 25 g/
1 oz/2 tablespoons of the remaining
butter until blended. Season to taste.
Spoon the mixture into a serving dish
and smooth the surface.
    Melt the remaining butter in a pan and
pour over the pâté. Place the bay leaf in
the centre, cover the pâté and leave in a
cool place until the butter has set. Serve
with bread or hot toast.
Prepare ahead. Cover the dish completely and chill in the refrigerator until
30 minutes before required.

Calamares salad

METRIC/IMPERIAL
700 g/1½ lb fresh squid
2 tablespoons olive oil
1 large onion, thinly sliced into rings
1 garlic clove, crushed
150 ml/¼ pint white wine
150 ml/¼ pint water
1 sprig fresh parsley
1 sprig fresh thyme
1 bay leaf
pinch each of dried marjoram and
    rosemary
1 strip of lemon peel
juice of ½ lemon
salt and pepper
1 tablespoon chopped fresh parsley to
    garnish

AMERICAN
1½ lb fresh squid
2 tablespoons olive oil
1 large onion, thinly sliced into rings
1 garlic clove, minced
⅔ cup white wine
⅔ cup water
1 sprig fresh parsley
1 sprig fresh thyme
1 bay leaf
pinch each of dried marjoram and
    rosemary
1 strip of lemon peel
juice of ½ lemon
salt and pepper
1 tablespoon chopped fresh parsley to
    garnish

Wash and skin the squid. Remove the long transparent backbone and clean the inside. Remove the head with its inkbags and push out the hard core from the centre of the tentacles. Cut the body into rings about 1.25 cm/½ inch wide. Leave the tentacles whole if they are quite small, otherwise cut them into 2.5 cm/ 1 inch lengths.

Heat the oil in a large saucepan, add the onion and garlic and cook for 1 minute. Add the squid, wine, water, fresh and dried herbs and the lemon peel. Bring to just under boiling point, cover and simmer for 1 hour or until the squid is tender.

Lift the squid out of the pan and put aside in a bowl. Boil the cooking liquid for 10 minutes to reduce slightly. Discard the parsley and thyme sprigs, lemon peel and bay leaf, then pour the liquid over the squid. Add the lemon juice and season to taste. Cool, cover and chill until 15 minutes before required. Sprinkle with the parsley and serve with fresh bread.

Prepare ahead. Cover the bowl and chill in the refrigerator until 15 minutes before required. Garnish and serve as above.

Freeze. Pour into a container, wrap, seal, label and freeze. Thaw overnight in the refrigerator or for 4 to 5 hours at room temperature.

Devilled prawns or shrimps

METRIC/IMPERIAL
2 tablespoons vegetable oil
1 large onion, finely chopped
1 garlic clove, crushed
500 g/1 lb tomatoes, peeled, quartered
    and seeded
1 tablespoon tomato purée
½ teaspoon sugar
½ teaspoon Tabasco sauce
2 teaspoons Worcestershire sauce
2 tablespoons lemon juice
salt and pepper
350 g/12 oz fresh peeled or frozen prawns
    or shrimps
1 tablespoon chopped fresh parsley to
garnish

Devilled prawns or shrimps

AMERICAN
2 tablespoons vegetable oil
1 large onion, finely chopped
1 garlic clove, minced
1 lb tomatoes, peeled, quartered and seeded
1 tablespoon tomato paste
½ teaspoon sugar
½ teaspoon Tabasco sauce
2 teaspoons Worcestershire sauce
2 tablespoons lemon juice
salt and pepper
1 lb fresh shelled or frozen small shrimp
1 tablespoon chopped fresh parsley to
    garnish

Heat the oil in a medium saucepan. Add the onion and garlic and fry gently for 5 minutes or until soft. Stir in the tomatoes, purée (paste), sugar, Tabasco, Worcestershire sauce, lemon juice and salt and pepper to taste. Bring to the boil, stirring, then lower the heat, half cover with a lid and simmer gently for 8 to 10 minutes or until the tomatoes are soft but still retain their shape. Stir in the prawns or shrimp(s) and heat through. Taste and correct seasoning if necessary. Serve immediately with boiled rice and sprinkle over the parsley.

Freeze. Wrap, seal, label and freeze the sauce. Thaw in a saucepan over low heat, stirring constantly, add the prawns or shrimp(s) and serve as above.

Coq au vin

METRIC/IMPERIAL
1.5 kg/3½ lb roasting chicken, jointed
50 g/2 oz flour
salt and pepper
50 g/2 oz butter

2 tablespoons oil
100 g/4 oz piece green bacon, rind
  removed and diced
500 kg/1 lb button onions, blanched and
  peeled
2 garlic cloves, crushed
1 tablespoon tomato purée
1 teaspoon sugar
2 tablespoons brandy
½ bottle full-bodied red wine
1 bouquet garni (parsley, marjoram and
  rosemary sprigs, 1 bay leaf)
225 g/8 oz button mushrooms
triangles of bread fried or toasted until
  crisp to garnish

AMERICAN
3½ lb roasting chicken, jointed
½ cup flour
salt and pepper
¼ cup butter
2 tablespoons oil
¼ lb piece bacon, rind removed and diced
1 lb baby white onions, blanched and
  peeled
2 garlic cloves, minced
1 tablespoon tomato paste
1 teaspoon sugar
2 tablespoons brandy
½ bottle full-bodied red wine
1 bouquet garni (parsley, marjoram and
  rosemary sprigs, 1 bay leaf)
2 cups small mushrooms
triangles of bread fried or toasted until
  crisp to garnish

Coat the chicken joints in the flour well
seasoned with salt and pepper. Heat the
butter and oil in a large saucepan. Add

Coq au vin

the chicken joints and brown quickly on
all sides. Remove the chicken joints as
they brown and set aside. Add the bacon,
onions and garlic and cook until golden
brown. Sprinkle in any remaining flour,
add the tomato purée (paste) and the
sugar and cook for 1 minute, stirring.

Return the chicken joints to the pan.
Warm the brandy, pour it over the
chicken and set alight. Allow to flame for
1 minute, then douse the flames with the
wine. Add the bouquet garni, cover the
pan and simmer gently for 30 to 40
minutes or until the chicken juices run
clear when the thick part of a joint is
pierced with a knife. Add the mushrooms
and simmer for a further 15 minutes.

Taste and adjust the seasoning if
necessary. Transfer the mixture to a
warmed casserole or deep dish, garnish
with the bread triangles and serve immediately with a green vegetable.

Prepare ahead. When the chicken is cooked, remove the pan from the heat and cool, transfer the mixture to a container, cover and chill in the refrigerator. Reheat the chicken mixture slowly until very hot, add the mushrooms and simmer for 15 minutes. Continue as above.

Freeze. Add the mushrooms, cool, wrap, seal, label and freeze. Thaw overnight in the refrigerator or for 4 to 5 hours at room temperature. Put in a saucepan and reheat gently, stirring occasionally, until very hot.

Red-cooked lamb

METRIC/IMPERIAL
2 tablespoons oil
1.25 kg/2½ lb shoulder of lamb, boned and cubed
salt and pepper
1 medium onion, chopped
1 garlic clove, crushed
3 tablespoons soy sauce
4 tablespoons dry sherry
2 teaspoons sugar
150 ml/¼ pint stock
1 tablespoon lemon juice
2.5 cm/1 inch piece root ginger, thinly sliced
2 bay leaves
2 teaspoons cornflour
1 red pepper, cored and sliced
AMERICAN
2 tablespoons oil
2½ lb boneless shoulder of lamb, cubed
salt and pepper
1 medium onion, chopped
1 garlic clove, minced
3 tablespoons soy sauce
4 tablespoons dry sherry
2 teaspoons sugar
⅔ cup stock
1 tablespoon lemon juice
1 inch piece root ginger, thinly sliced
2 bay leaves
2 teaspoons cornstarch
1 red pepper, cored and sliced

Heat the oil in a large saucepan, add the meat, season well, and cook quickly until browned on all sides. As the meat browns remove it to a casserole. Add the onion and garlic to the pan and cook for 7 minutes or until golden brown. Stir in the soy sauce, sherry, sugar, stock and lemon juice and bring to the boil. Pour over the meat, add the ginger and bay leaves, cover and cook in a moderate oven, 180°C/350°F, Gas Mark 4 for 1 to

1¼ hours or until the meat is tender. Half an hour before the end of cooking time stir in the cornflour (cornstarch) mixed to a smooth paste with a little water and continue cooking. Remove and discard the bay leaves. Serve the meat very hot, sprinkled with the red pepper, and accompanied by boiled rice, prawn crackers and extra soy sauce if liked.
Prepare ahead. Cook the meat, cool, cover and chill until required. Place the mixture in a large saucepan and bring to the boil, stirring. Lower the heat and

Red-cooked lamb

simmer gently for 10 minutes or until heated through. Serve as above with the pepper.
Freeze. Cook until meat is tender, don't add cornflour (cornstarch). Wrap, seal, label and freeze. Thaw overnight in refrigerator or for 4 hours at room temperature. Reheat in a saucepan, stirring occasionally, until hot, stir in the cornflour (cornstarch) mixture and continue as above.

Topside braise

METRIC/IMPERIAL
1 kg/2 lb beef topside
salt and pepper
25 g/1 oz lard or dripping
½ teaspoon dried mixed herbs
225 g/8 oz carrots, sliced
2 large onions, sliced
300 ml/½ pint brown ale
1 tablespoon cornflour
AMERICAN
2 lb beef rump or round
salt and pepper
2 tablespoons lard or drippings
½ teaspoon dried mixed herbs
1 cup sliced carrots
2 large onions, sliced
1¼ cups beer
1 tablespoon cornstarch

Place the meat on a board and rub in a generous quantity of seasoning. Heat the fat in a baking tin and brown the meat quickly on all sides. Sprinkle over the herbs and place the carrots and onions in the fat around the meat. Place in a moderately hot oven, 200°C/400°F, Gas Mark 6 for 30 minutes. Pour the beer over the meat, reduce the heat to moderate, 180°C/350°F, Gas Mark 4 and cook for a further 45 minutes or until the meat is cooked but still slightly pink in the centre.

Transfer the meat to a board and carve into thick slices. Place on a warmed serving dish and keep warm while making the gravy.

Using a slotted spoon transfer the vegetables to the serving dish and arrange around the meat; keep warm. Pour the cooking juices into a small saucepan. Mix the cornflour (cornstarch) to a smooth paste with a little water and stir into the gravy. Bring to the boil, stirring, and cook for 1 minute or until the gravy has thickened. Pour over the meat and vegetables and serve immediately with mashed potatoes and Brussels sprouts.

Prepare ahead. Place the slices of meat in a container and cover with the vegetables and cooking juices, cover and chill until required. Place in a baking tin and reheat in a moderately hot oven, 190°C/375°F, Gas Mark 5 for 25 minutes or until bubbling. Transfer to a serving dish and thicken juices as above.

Topside braise

Freeze. Place the slices of meat in a container and cover with the vegetables and cooking juices, cover, seal, label and freeze. Thaw overnight in the refrigerator or for 4 hours at room temperature. Reheat in a saucepan until hot, place meat and vegetables on a warmed serving dish. Thicken cooking juices and serve as above.

Ratatouille

METRIC/IMPERIAL
1 large aubergine, sliced
salt and pepper
4 tablespoons olive oil
2 medium onions, thinly sliced
1 garlic clove, crushed
700 g/1½ lb tomatoes, peeled, seeded and quartered
500 g/1 lb courgettes, sliced
1 large green pepper, cored, seeded and thinly sliced
1 large red pepper, cored, seeded and thinly sliced
½ teaspoon dried oregano
AMERICAN
1 large eggplant, sliced
salt and pepper
4 tablespoons olive oil
2 medium onions, thinly sliced
1 garlic clove, minced
1½ lb tomatoes, peeled, seeded and quartered
1 lb zucchini, sliced
1 large green pepper, cored, seeded and thinly sliced
1 large red pepper, cored, seeded and thinly sliced
½ teaspoon dried oregano

Sprinkle the aubergine (eggplant) slices with salt and leave to drain in a colander for 30 minutes. Wash off the salt and dry the slices with absorbent kitchen paper.

Heat the oil in a frying pan (skillet), add the onions, garlic and tomatoes and cook gently for 4 minutes, stirring, until the tomatoes soften. Add the courgettes (zucchini), peppers, aubergine (eggplant) and oregano and salt and pepper to taste. Bring the mixture to the boil, stirring, cover and simmer for 30 minutes or until the vegetables are soft. Serve immediately as a side dish with roast lamb. Alternatively allow to cool and serve cold as a starter.

Prepare ahead. Cook until the vegetables are tender, transfer to a container, cool, cover and chill in the refrigerator. Re-move 30 minutes before required, if serving cold, and transfer to a shallow serving dish. To serve hot, transfer the mixture to a saucepan and bring to the boil. Simmer gently, stirring occasionally, for 5 minutes or until very hot.

Freeze. Wrap, seal, label and freeze. Thaw for 4 to 5 hours at room temperature if serving cold. If serving hot, reheat from frozen in a saucepan, adding a little water if necessary, until hot.

Courgette (zucchini) ragoût

METRIC/IMPERIAL
25 g/1 oz butter
1 tablespoon oil
2 medium onions, chopped
1 garlic clove, crushed
700 g/1½ lb courgettes, peeled and sliced
225 g/8 oz tomatoes, peeled and roughly chopped
salt and pepper
4 eggs, lightly beaten
AMERICAN
2 tablespoons butter
1 tablespoon oil
2 medium onions, chopped
1 garlic clove, minced
1½ lb zucchini, peeled and sliced
1 cup peeled and roughly chopped tomatoes
salt and pepper
4 eggs, lightly beaten

Heat the butter and oil in a saucepan, add the onions and garlic and cook for 5 minutes or until soft. Add the slices of courgette (zucchini), tomatoes and seasoning to taste. Cover and simmer for 20 to 30 minutes or until the courgettes (zucchini) are tender.

Stir in the eggs and cook over very low heat, stirring, until lightly set. Serve immediately with hot toast or jacket potatoes as a light main course.

Note: If the eggs are omitted the dish may be served as a vegetable side dish with hamburgers or grilled (broiled) gammon.

Illustrated overleaf: Courgette (zucchini) ragoût

Onions braised in cider

METRIC/IMPERIAL
2 tablespoons oil
4–6 large onions, preferably Spanish
300 ml/½ pint dry cider
1 bay leaf
1 sprig sage or ¼ teaspoon dried sage
salt and pepper
AMERICAN
2 tablespoons oil
4–6 large onions, preferably Bermuda
1¼ cups hard cider
1 bay leaf
1 sprig sage or ¼ teaspoon dried sage
salt and pepper

Heat the oil in a saucepan large enough to hold the onions side by side. Add the onions and pour over the cider. Add the bay leaf, sage and salt and pepper to taste, half cover the pan and simmer for 30 minutes or until the onions are tender.

Transfer the onions to a warmed dish, keep warm. Boil the cooking liquid rapidly until reduced to a thin, syrupy consistency. Strain over the onions and serve hot, with roast lamb or pork.

Mushrooms in soured cream

METRIC/IMPERIAL
50 g/2 oz butter
2 medium onions, finely chopped
500 g/1 lb button mushrooms, thinly
    sliced
1 teaspoon lemon juice
½ teaspoon dried basil
150 ml/¼ pint cultured soured cream
salt and pepper
AMERICAN
¼ cup butter
2 medium onions, finely chopped
1 lb small mushrooms, thinly sliced
1 teaspoon lemon juice
½ teaspoon dried basil
⅔ cup sour cream
salt and pepper

Melt the butter in a saucepan, add the onions and cook gently until soft but not brown. Add the mushrooms, lemon juice

Onions braised in cider; Courgette (zucchini) ragoût (page 93); Mushrooms in soured cream

and basil. Cook, uncovered, over a low heat for 10 minutes or until the mushrooms are soft and the liquid has evaporated. Stir in the sour(ed) cream, season to taste and heat without boiling until hot. Serve immediately with fried steak, meat patties or lamb chops.

Indian cauliflower

METRIC/IMPERIAL
1 small onion, quartered
3 garlic cloves, peeled
25 g/1 oz fresh root ginger, peeled and roughly chopped
4 tablespoons water
4 tablespoons oil
½ teaspoon ground turmeric
2 tomatoes, peeled and chopped
¼ teaspoon cayenne pepper
1 teaspoon ground cumin
1 teaspoon ground cinnamon
2 teaspoons salt
pepper
juice of ½ lemon
1 cauliflower, divided into florets
150 ml/¼ pint unsweetened yogurt

AMERICAN
1 small onion, quartered
3 garlic cloves, peeled
2 inch piece of fresh root ginger, peeled and roughly chopped
4 tablespoons water
4 tablespoons oil
½ teaspoon ground turmeric
2 tomatoes, peeled and chopped
¼ teaspoon cayenne pepper
1 teaspoon ground cumin
1 teaspoon ground cinnamon
2 teaspoons salt
pepper
juice of ½ lemon
1 cauliflower, divided into florets
⅔ cup unsweetened yogurt

Put the onion, garlic, ginger and water into an electric blender and purée until smooth. Alternatively chop the ingredients very finely. Heat the oil in a saucepan, add the onion mixture, the turmeric, tomatoes, cayenne, cumin, cinnamon, salt and pepper to taste. Cook for 5 minutes, stirring, adding a little water if the mixture begins to stick to the bottom of the pan. Add the lemon juice and the cauliflower and stir to coat the cauliflower with the sauce. Cover the pan and cook gently for 15 to 20 minutes or until the cauliflower is just tender. Add the yogurt and adjust the seasoning. Transfer the mixture to a warm dish and serve with grilled (broiled) lamb or pork chops.

Broccoli in cheese sauce

METRIC/IMPERIAL
700 g/1½ lb fresh broccoli, divided into florets, or 2 × 283 g/10 oz packets frozen broccoli
salt and pepper
25 g/1 oz butter
25 g/1 oz flour
300 ml/½ pint milk
¼ teaspoon dry mustard
50 g/2 oz Cheddar cheese, grated
1 tablespoon dried breadcrumbs
15 g/½ oz butter, cut into small pieces
AMERICAN
1½ lb bunch fresh broccoli, divided into florets, or 2 × 10 oz packages frozen broccoli spears
salt and pepper
2 tablespoons butter
¼ cup flour
1¼ cups milk
¼ teaspoon dry mustard
½ cup grated Cheddar cheese
1 tablespoon dried breadcrumbs
1 tablespoon butter, cut into small pieces

Cook the broccoli in the minimum of boiling salted water for 10 to 15 minutes or until just tender. Transfer to a warm ovenproof dish and reserve the cooking liquid.

Melt the butter in a saucepan, add the flour and cook for 1 minute. Gradually add the milk, stirring constantly, and bring to the boil, still stirring. Stir in 1 tablespoon of the reserved cooking liquid and simmer for 2 minutes. Stir in the mustard, half the grated cheese and salt and pepper to taste. Pour the sauce over the broccoli. Mix together the remaining cheese and the breadcrumbs and sprinkle over the sauce. Dot the top with the butter and place under a hot grill (broiler) until the top is golden brown and bubbling.

Serve immediately as a supper dish or as an accompaniment to roast pork or veal escalope.

Broccoli in cheese sauce; Indian cauliflower

Austrian red cabbage

METRIC/IMPERIAL
1 small red cabbage, thinly sliced
1 large onion, thinly sliced
1 large cooking apple, peeled, cored and
  sliced
4 tablespoons chicken stock
2 tablespoons wine or cider vinegar
1 tablespoon sugar
3 whole cloves, crushed
$\frac{1}{4}$ teaspoon grated nutmeg
salt and pepper
15 g/$\frac{1}{2}$ oz butter

AMERICAN
1 small red cabbage, shredded
1 large onion, thinly sliced
1 large cooking apple, peeled, cored and
  sliced
4 tablespoons chicken stock
2 tablespoons wine or cider vinegar
1 tablespoon sugar
3 whole cloves, minced
$\frac{1}{4}$ teaspoon grated nutmeg
salt and pepper
1 tablespoon butter

Put the cabbage, onion and apple in a large casserole. Pour in the stock and vinegar and sprinkle over the sugar, cloves, nutmeg and salt and pepper to taste. Stir well to mix.

Cover the casserole and bake in a moderate oven, 180°C/350°F, Gas Mark 4 for 1 to 1$\frac{1}{2}$ hours or until the cabbage is very tender. Taste and adjust the seasoning if necessary. Stir in the butter and serve immediately with grilled (broiled) or roast pork or, more simply, with grilled (broiled) English or Continental sausages.

Prepare ahead. When the cabbage is tender, cool, cover and chill in the refrigerator until required. Reheat the cabbage in a moderate oven for 30 to 40 minutes, or until very hot, stirring in the butter halfway through. Alternatively, transfer the cabbage mixture to a saucepan, add the butter and reheat, stirring, until the mixture is hot, cover the pan and simmer for 5 minutes.

Swiss-style potato cake

METRIC/IMPERIAL
1 kg/2 lb potatoes, boiled in their jackets
  for 10 minutes, drained, cooled and
  peeled
50 g/2 oz Gruyère or Cheddar cheese,
  grated
75 g/3 oz butter
1 medium onion, finely chopped
salt and pepper
2 slices cooked ham, chopped
sprig of parsley to garnish

Swiss-style potato cake

AMERICAN
2 lb potatoes, boiled in their skins for 10
  minutes, drained, cooled and peeled
$\frac{1}{2}$ cup grated Gruyère or Cheddar cheese
$\frac{1}{3}$ cup butter
1 medium onion, finely chopped
salt and pepper
2 slices cooked ham, chopped
sprig of parsley to garnish

Grate the potatoes into a large bowl, and stir in the cheese. Melt 1 tablespoon of the butter in a frying pan (skillet), when foaming, add the onion and cook for 7 minutes or until soft and golden. Add to the potato mixture and add salt and pepper to taste. Melt the remaining butter, add the potato mixture and press into a flat cake. Sprinkle the ham on top. Cook for 5 minutes on each side or until golden brown and cooked through.

Invert the potato cake onto a warm serving dish and garnish with parsley. Serve with sausages or fried eggs for a complete meal. Alternatively serve as a side dish with grilled (broiled) or roast meat.

Prepare ahead. Cook the potato cake in half of the remaining butter on one side for 5 minutes or until golden brown. Invert the cake onto a large piece of aluminium foil, cover completely and chill in the refrigerator until required. Melt the remaining butter in the pan, add the potato cake unbrowned side downwards and cook for 10 to 15 minutes or until golden brown and heated through.

Bean salad

METRIC/IMPERIAL
500 g/1 lb French or runner beans, fresh
  or frozen
salt and pepper
1 small onion, very finely chopped
1 tablespoon white wine vinegar
3 tablespoons oil
1 teaspoon lemon juice
$\frac{1}{4}$ teaspoon sugar
$\frac{1}{2}$ teaspoon dried or fresh marjoram

AMERICAN
1 lb French-style green beans, fresh or
  frozen
salt and pepper
1 small onion, very finely chopped
1 tablespoon white wine vinegar
3 tablespoons oil
1 teaspoon lemon juice
$\frac{1}{4}$ teaspoon sugar
$\frac{1}{2}$ teaspoon dried or fresh marjoram

Cook the beans in boiling salted water for 5 to 10 minutes or until just tender. Drain and place in a salad bowl. Sprinkle over the onion. Whisk together the vinegar, oil, lemon juice, salt and pepper to taste, sugar and marjoram to make a dressing. Pour over the beans, mix well and leave until completely cold. Chill until 30 minutes before required.

Serve as a side dish with moussaka or lasagne or as one of a selection of salads for a first course.

Coleslaw

METRIC/IMPERIAL
½ *small white cabbage, finely sliced*
4 stalks celery, chopped
1 medium onion, very finely chopped
4 large carrots, grated
salt and pepper
4 tablespoons mayonnaise
1 tablespoon lemon juice
1 red-skinned apple
25 g/1 oz shelled walnuts, chopped
1 orange, peeled and separated into
  segments
AMERICAN
½ *small white cabbage, shredded*
4 stalks celery, chopped
1 medium onion, very finely chopped
4 large carrots, grated
salt and pepper
4 tablespoons mayonnaise
1 tablespoon lemon juice
1 red-skinned apple
¼ *cup shelled chopped walnuts*
1 orange, peeled and separated into
  segments

Put the cabbage, celery, onion, carrots and seasoning to taste in a large bowl and mix well. Stir in the mayonnaise and lemon juice until the vegetables are well coated. If liked, cover the bowl and chill until required.

Stir in the apple, walnuts and orange just before serving. This is a popular salad to serve with cold meat, cheese or savoury flans.

Coleslaw preparation

Caesar salad

METRIC/IMPERIAL
225 g/8 oz chicory
½ small cucumber, sliced
6 radishes, chopped
2 spring onions, chopped
3 sliced bread, cubed
1 egg, beaten
25 g/1 oz Parmesan cheese, grated
½ teaspoon dry mustard
1 tablespoon oil
25 g/1 oz butter
1 garlic clove, crushed
AMERICAN
½ lb endive
½ small cucumber, sliced
6 radishes, chopped
2 scallions, chopped
3 slices bread, cubed
1 egg, beaten
¼ cup grated Parmesan cheese
½ teaspoon dry mustard
1 tablespoon oil
2 tablespoons butter
1 garlic clove, minced

Arrange the chicory (endive) around the edge of a serving dish, arrange the cucumber in a circle inside and fill the middle with the radishes and spring onions (scallions).

Coat the bread cubes in beaten egg. Mix the Parmesan and mustard together and coat the bread cubes. Heat the oil and butter together in a frying pan (skillet), add the garlic and stir well. Add the bread cubes and fry until golden brown and crisp. Drain the cubes on absorbent kitchen paper and allow to cool. Pile the cubes on top of the radishes and onions. Serve as a crisp and tasty starter.

Leek salad

METRIC/IMPERIAL
350 g/12 oz leeks (white and pale green parts only), sliced
salt and pepper
150 ml/¼ pint cultured soured cream
1 garlic clove, crushed
1 teaspoon creamed horseradish
1 teaspoon brown sugar
2 tablespoons lemon juice
1 tablespoon vegetable oil

AMERICAN
¾ lb leeks (white and pale green parts only), sliced
salt and pepper
⅔ cup sour cream
1 garlic clove, minced
1 teaspoon creamed horseradish
1 teaspoon brown sugar
2 tablespoons lemon juice
1 tablespoon vegetable oil

Cook the leeks in the minimum of boiling salted water for 5 minutes or until just starting to soften. Drain, rinse with cold water and drain again, very thoroughly. Place in a deep serving dish. Mix together the sour(ed) cream, garlic, horseradish, sugar, lemon juice, oil and salt and pepper to taste and beat well. Pour over the leeks and leave for at least 1 hour in a cool place.

Stir the salad well before serving with cold meat or quiche. Alternatively, serve as a first course accompanied by other salads.

Curried corn salad

METRIC/IMPERIAL
500 g/1 lb sweetcorn kernels, cooked
1 medium onion, finely chopped
2 tablespoons mayonnaise
2 tablespoons fresh single cream
1 tablespoon lemon juice
1 tablespoon apricot jam
salt and pepper
2 teaspoons paprika
1 tablespoon mild curry powder
1 garlic clove, crushed
1 tablespoon chopped fresh parsley
AMERICAN
3 cups kernel corn, cooked
1 medium onion, finely chopped
2 tablespoons mayonnaise
2 tablespoons light cream
1 tablespoon lemon juice
1 tablespoon apricot jam
salt and pepper
2 teaspoons paprika
1 tablespoon mild curry powder
1 garlic clove, minced
1 tablespoon chopped fresh parsley

Place the sweetcorn kernels and onion in a bowl. Beat together the mayonnaise, cream, lemon juice, jam, salt and pepper to taste, paprika, curry powder, garlic and half the parsley. Pour over the vegetables and mix well. Turn into a

serving dish, cover and chill for 30 minutes. Serve the salad garnished with the remaining parsley.

Prepare ahead. Transfer the mixture to a container, cover and chill in the refrigerator until 15 minutes before required. Spoon into a serving dish and serve as above.

French bean and orange salad

METRIC/IMPERIAL
500 g/1 lb French beans
salt
3 oranges
½ cucumber
Dressing:
150 ml/¼ pint mayonnaise
1 tablespoon chopped stuffed olives
1 tablespoon chopped onion
1 egg, hard-boiled and chopped
1 tablespoon chopped capers
1 teaspoon chopped fresh parsley
1 teaspoon tomato purée
AMERICAN
1 lb French-style green beans
salt
3 oranges
½ cucumber
Dressing:
⅔ cup mayonnaise
1 tablespoon chopped pimiento-stuffed olives
1 tablespoon chopped onion
1 hard-cooked egg, chopped
1 tablespoon chopped capers
1 teaspoon chopped fresh parsley
1 teaspoon tomato paste

Cook the beans in boiling salted water for 5 minutes or until just tender. Drain. Remove the skin and pith from the oranges and separate into segments. Pile the beans in the centre of a serving plate and arrange orange segments and cucumber slices alternately around the outside.

Mix all the dressing ingredients together and serve with the salad. Serve as a piquant first course or serve as a side salad with cold meat.

Grapefruit and grape salad

METRIC/IMPERIAL
4 large grapefruit
100 g/4 oz green grapes, halved and pips removed
50 g/2 oz Brazil nuts, roughly chopped
25 g/1 oz hazelnuts, halved
Dressing:
4 tablespoons wine vinegar
6 tablespoons olive oil
2 teaspoons sugar
1 teaspoon French mustard
salt and pepper
3 tablespoons fresh single cream
AMERICAN
4 large grapefruit
1 cup white grapes, halved and seeds removed
½ cup chopped Brazil nuts
¼ cup halved hazelnuts
Dressing:
4 tablespoons wine vinegar
6 tablespoons olive oil
2 teaspoons sugar
1 teaspoon French mustard
salt and pepper
3 tablespoons light cream

Remove the skin and white pith from the grapefruit, separate into segments and place in a bowl. Add the grapes and nuts. Put the dressing ingredients in a bowl and beat until well mixed. Pour the dressing over the grapefruit and transfer to a serving bowl. Serve as a starter.
Prepare ahead. Cover and chill in the refrigerator until 15 minutes before required.
Note. This salad can be served as a dessert, without the dressing.

Waldorf salad; Grapefruit and grape salad

Waldorf salad

METRIC/IMPERIAL
500 g/1 lb eating apples
juice of 1 lemon
150 ml/¼ pint mayonnaise
½ head celery, chopped
25 g/1 oz walnuts, chopped
salt and pepper
1 lettuce
AMERICAN
1 lb dessert apples
juice of 1 lemon
⅔ cup mayonnaise
½ bunch celery, chopped
¼ cup chopped walnuts
salt and pepper
1 lettuce

Peel and core the apples. Cut the apples into large dice and toss in the lemon juice to prevent them turning brown. Add the mayonnaise, celery, walnuts, and seasoning to taste and stir well until mixed.

Arrange lettuce leaves on a serving dish and pile the salad on top.
Prepare ahead. Make the apple mixture, transfer to a container and chill in the refrigerator until required. Arrange lettuce on a dish, stir the salad to mix thoroughly and serve on the lettuce.

Apricot shortcake

METRIC/IMPERIAL
225 g/8 oz self-raising flour
½ teaspoon ground ginger
½ teaspoon salt
75 g/3 oz butter, cut into small pieces
75 g/3 oz sugar
1 egg, beaten
1–2 tablespoons milk
500 g/1 lb apricots, halved and stoned
3 tablespoons sugar
300 ml/½ pint fresh double cream, lightly beaten

AMERICAN

2 cups flour sifted with 2 teaspoons
   baking powder
$\frac{1}{2}$ teaspoon ground ginger
$\frac{1}{4}$ teaspoon salt
$\frac{1}{4}$ cup butter, cut into small pieces
$\frac{1}{3}$ cup sugar
1 egg, beaten
1–2 tablespoons milk
1 lb apricots, halved and pitted
3 tablespoons sugar
$1\frac{1}{4}$ cups heavy cream, lightly beaten

Sift the flour, ginger and salt into a mixing bowl. Add the butter and rub in until the mixture resembles fine bread-crumbs. Stir in the sugar, egg and enough of the milk to make a very stiff dough. Knead lightly and roll out to a circle to fit a 20 cm/8 inch loose-bottomed cake tin (springform pan). Press into the tin (pan) and chill in the refrigerator for 30 minutes.

Meanwhile, stew the apricots, cov-ered, in very little water with the 3 tablespoons sugar for 10 to 12 minutes or until they are just tender and still whole. Cool. Drain apricots.

Bake the shortcake in a moderately hot oven, 190°C/375°F, Gas Mark 5 for 20 minutes or until golden brown and set. Cool for 10 minutes, then remove from the tin (pan) and cool on a wire rack. When cold, split the cake in two. Spread half the shortcake with half the cream and place two-thirds of the apricots on top. Cover with the other shortcake half, spread with the remain-ing cream and decorate with the remain-ing apricots. Serve immediately if you like the shortcake to be crisp; leave in a cool place for up to 1 hour if you like it slightly softer.
Prepare ahead. Bake the shortcake, cool completely, wrap in aluminium foil and keep until required. Poach the apricots, cool in cooking juices, cover and chill until required. Drain apricots and as-semble cake when required.

Serves 4–6.

Melon and grape jelly

METRIC/IMPERIAL

1 melon, halved and seeded
2 dessert apples, peeled, cored and sliced
grated rind and juice of 2 limes or lemons
175 g/6 oz black grapes, halved and pips
   removed
15 g/$\frac{1}{2}$ oz powdered gelatine
2 tablespoons water
4 tablespoons clear honey

AMERICAN

1 melon, halved and seeded
2 dessert apples, peeled, cored and sliced
grated rind and juice of 2 limes or lemons
$1\frac{1}{2}$ cups black grapes, halved and seeded
2 envelopes unflavored gelatin
2 tablespoons water
4 tablespoons clear honey

Scoop the melon flesh into balls and mix with the apples, lime or lemon juice and rind and grapes. Scoop out the remain-ing melon flesh, chop roughly and add to fruit mixture. Sprinkle the gelatin(e) over the water in a small bowl and leave for 5 minutes. Place in a pan of hot water and heat gently until dissolved. Stir in the honey and pour over the fruit mix-ture, stirring well to mix. Spoon the fruit mixture into the melon halves and leave in a cool place to set.

Cut the melon halves into quarters, or smaller, and serve with cream, if liked.
Prepare ahead. Leave to set. Cover closely with plastic wrap and then with aluminium foil and chill in the refriger-ator until 15 minutes before required. Cut into portions.

Serves 4–6.

Apricot shortcake

Savarin

METRIC/IMPERIAL
25 g/1 oz fresh yeast
6 tablespoons warm milk
40 g/1½ oz caster sugar
225 g/8 oz strong white plain flour
½ teaspoon salt
4 eggs, beaten
50 g/2 oz butter, softened
Syrup:
350 g/12 oz sugar
350 ml/12 fl oz water
4–6 tablespoons rum
Glaze:
3 tablespoons apricot jam, sieved
1 tablespoon water
Filling:
225 g/8 oz strawberries, halved
100 g/4 oz green grapes, halved and pips
   removed
2–3 slices fresh or canned pineapple, cut
   into cubes

AMERICAN
1 cake compressed yeast
6 tablespoons warm milk
3 tablespoons sugar
2 cups flour
½ teaspoon salt
4 eggs, beaten
¼ cup butter, softened
Syrup:
1½ cups sugar
1½ cups water
4–6 tablespoons rum
Glaze:
3 tablespoons apricot jam, sieved
1 tablespoon water
Filling:
1½ cups strawberries, halved
1 cup white grapes, halved and seeded
2–3 slices fresh or canned pineapple, cut
   into cubes

Mix the yeast with the milk until smooth, stir in 1 teaspoon of the sugar and 50 g/ 2 oz/½ cup of the flour and leave in a warm place for 15 minutes or until frothy.

Sift the remaining flour and the salt into a warmed mixing bowl and stir in the remaining sugar. Make a well in the centre and pour in the eggs and the yeast mixture. Add the softened butter and, stirring with a wooden spoon, gradually draw all the ingredients together. Beat vigorously for 3 to 4 minutes or until the mixture is smooth and elastic.

Pour the batter into a greased 23 cm/ 9 inch savarin tin (pan) or ring mould and place inside an oiled polythene (plastic) bag. Leave in a warm place for 30 to 40 minutes or until the dough has risen to the top of the tin (pan) or mould. Remove from the bag and bake in a moderately hot oven, 200°C/400°F, Gas Mark 6 for 25 minutes or until set and golden brown.

Meanwhile, prepare the syrup. Dissolve the sugar in the water, stirring over gentle heat. Bring to the boil and boil for 1 minute. Remove the pan from the heat and stir in the rum to taste.

Allow the savarin to cool for 5 minutes. Make skewer holes over the surface of the savarin and spoon the syrup into the holes until it has soaked in as much as it will take. Leave to cool completely. Turn out onto a serving dish.

For the glaze, warm the apricot jam and water together until hot and well mixed and brush over the surface of the savarin. If any syrup remains mix with the fruit. Pile the fruit in the centre of the savarin and serve with cream.

Prepare ahead. Cook the savarin and soak with the syrup. Cool completely and turn out onto the serving dish. Cover with the mould to prevent drying, and chill until 45 minutes before required. Remove mould and finish as above.

Serves 4–6.

Savarin

Index

Acknowledgements

The publishers would like to thank the following individuals and organizations for their kind permission to reproduce the photographs in this book:

Rex Bamber: 11, 12, 14-15, 19, 21, 22, 26, 56, 62, 64, 75, 80, 82, 97-101; Bisto: 40, 45, 48, 52; Colmans Mustard: 53; Dutch Dairy Bureau: 17, 33; Flour Advisory Bureau: 102; Gales Honey: 70; Melvin Grey: 30, 43, 57, 59, 69, 72, 86, 88, 89, 95, 96; Paul Kemp: 16, 18, 23, 25, 28-29, 32, 34, 35, 39, 41, 47, 49, 61, 63, 78-79, 83, 84, 90-94; Knorr Stock Cubes: 36-37, 54; Mike Leale: 51; David Levin: 1-9; Mattesons: 85; Olives from Spain: 20, 74, 76; Prestige: 38; Taunton Cider: 44; Van den Berghs: 66; White Fish Authority: 24.

The publishers also wish to thank the following companies for the loan of accessories for photography:

The Craftsmen Potters Shop; Dickens & Jones; Peter Jones.

PDO 79-178